THE **MINI** ROUGH GUIDE TO
BUCHAREST

ROUGH
GUIDES

YOUR TAILOR-MADE TRIP
STARTS HERE

Tailor-made trips and unique adventures crafted by local experts

HOW ROUGHGUIDES.COM/TRIPS WORKS

STEP 1

Pick your dream destination, tell us what you want and submit an enquiry.

STEP 2

Fill in a short form to tell your local expert about your dream trip and preferences.

STEP 3

Our local expert will craft your tailor-made itinerary. You'll be able to tweak and refine it until you're completely satisfied.

STEP 4

Book online with ease, pack your bags and enjoy the trip! Our local expert will be on hand 24/7 while you're on the road.

PLAN AND BOOK YOUR TRIP AT
ROUGHGUIDES.COM/TRIPS

HOW TO DOWNLOAD
YOUR FREE EBOOK

1. Visit **www.roughguides.com/
   free-ebook** or scan the **QR
   code** opposite

2. Enter the code **bucharest071**

3. Follow the simple step-by-step
   instructions

For troubleshooting contact: mail@roughguides.com

10 THINGS NOT TO MISS

1

2

3

4

5

6

7

A PERFECT DAY

9.00am

Covrigi and coffee. Queue up for pretzel-like covrigi at any branch of Luca, Romania's favourite bakery chain, then enjoy coffee with a book at the Old Town's Carusel Café.

10.00am

Old Town. Wander the streets of the Old Town and admire the eclectic architecture before the lunchtime crowds descend on the area.

11.00am

Parliament. Take the guided tour of Romania's largest building, making sure you grab some perfect shots of the city centre from the balcony.

12.30pm

Caru cu Bere. Try some traditional Romanian food in this historic restaurant (see page 103) – the interior is a must-see.

1.30pm

Calea Victoriei. Stroll along the city's finest street, taking in the sights of the 1989 revolution and the many historical buildings, including the former Royal Palace, as well as browsing its high-end shops.

IN **BUCHAREST**

2.30pm

Village Museum. Explore the many houses, churches, windmills and farm buildings that showcase the inventive spirit of the Romanian people, and pick up some handmade, traditional crafts in the museum shop.

4.00pm

Spring Palace. Remain aghast at the kitsch opulence in which Romania's communist leaders lived while the rest of the country went hungry.

6.00pm

A concert at the Ateneul Român. See one of Europe's finest orchestras, the George Enescu Philharmonic, perform at one of the continent's most lavish concert halls.

8.30pm

The Artist. Finish the day with dinner at Romania's best restaurant (see page 106), before heading to Piaţa Unirii to watch the spectacular dancing fountains.

CONTENTS

OVERVIEW

Bucharest's locals love nothing more than teasing visitors from other parts of Romania, and will often do so by declaring – with tongue only partly in cheek – that the capital is the country's only city. 'Everything else is just a big village', they say, and they are at least partially right: with an official population of just under 2 million (and an unofficial population higher than that), Bucharest is four times larger than any other city in the country, and – in what remains a highly-centralised state – the focal point of Romanian politics, business, culture, religion and sport. For the visitor, it is an often bewildering mix of the Western and the Oriental, the modern and the traditional. This city of extremes, where state-of-the-art Teslas must navigate potholed roads, may frustrate and delight in equal measure. Badly administered for decades, it creaks and often appears on the verge of collapsing entirely, but has enough charm and attractions to make it an appealing destination for all but the most jaded traveller.

GEOGRAPHY

Historically, Romania was divided into three principalities: Wallachia, the area north of the Danube; Transylvania (or Ardeal), west of the Carpathians; and Moldavia in the north, the eastern part of which is today the Republic of Moldova. Largely flat and with few natural landmarks, set in the heart of the great Wallachian plain about 60km (37 miles) north of the Danube, the extent of Bucharest's urban sprawl is visible from miles away – long before your plane lands at Henri Coanda International Airport. Although still filled with concrete monstrosities built before (and, in some cases, after) the fall of the Berlin Wall, it's a surprisingly green city: large parks and public gardens abound, although during the hot summer this matters little as its streets can be dusty and suffocating. Bucharest lacks a real centre or focal point, though one could make an argument for Piața Unirii, where three of the city's five metro lines converge.

CONTEMPORARY BUCHAREST AND ITS PEOPLE

During Romania's communist period it was a privilege to live in Bucharest. A *buletin de Bucuresti,* which conferred residence rights on those lucky enough to possess one, became a sought-after item, so much so that in the 1970s a comedy film was made about one man's Kafka-esque quest to procure such a document. These days, anyone can move to the capital, and each year thousands do. A vast business district in the northern Pipera district has seen innumerable skyscrapers spring up to house the international

Basarab Overpass.

companies that employ the country's most talented young people. As such, Bucharest remains a magnet for Romanians in search of fame and fortune, even though it must now compete with the attraction of emigration. Locals are far friendlier (at least to foreigners) than other Romanians would have you believe, and almost everyone under the age of 40 will speak at least a smattering of English. Most are fluent.

CLIMATE

In keeping with the 'land of extremes' theme, Bucharest has uncomfortably hot summers and very cold winters, with little in between. Temperatures in July and August often top 35°C (95°F), and in

RELIGION

The overwhelming majority of the Romanian population, around 87 percent, is Orthodox Christian. In Bucharest the percentage is higher still. There is a significant Catholic minority in Transylvania, especially among the Hungarian population, while Protestants also make up a significant minority amongst the Saxon population of Transylvania. The current president, Klaus Iohannis, is Lutheran. Faith amongst Bucharest's locals is strong; note how many Romanians ostentatiously cross themselves while passing a church on a bus, or tram. This faith is particularly visible at Easter, when it can appear that the entire city descends on its many churches for midnight Mass. Most are forced to listen to the service outside, as the churches are full. For the visitor, Easter is a wonderful opportunity to see just how devout Romanians have remained, despite the attempts of the communist regime to erode the influence of the church. It's a genuinely collective cultural experience you will not forget.

Downtown Bucharest in the snow.

winter can stay below freezing for weeks, sometimes even months, on end. Snow regularly covers the ground for long periods, but locals are a hardy bunch: the city does not grind to a halt at the first dusting of the white stuff. If you are looking for a white Christmas, Bucharest is a decent place to come. May and June are traditionally very wet, but the downpours – while violent and often capable of flooding streets in just a few minutes – never last too long.

BUCHAREST'S ATTRACTIONS

Not a particularly old city – it was founded only in the mid-15th century – Bucharest nevertheless packs a historical punch. The 1989 revolution usually takes top billing; numerous tours now take visitors around the sights of that brief but bloody conflict, when forces loyal to the dictator Nicolae Ceaușescu fought with those who wished to depose him. While the communist regime flattened much of the old city to make way for Ceaușescu's megalomaniac

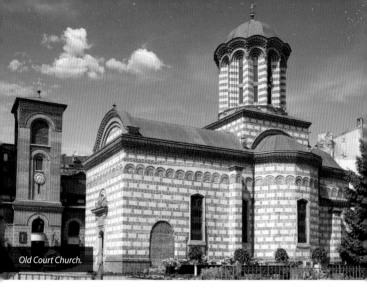

Old Court Church.

vision of a new city for a new, communist man – of which the enormous parliament building is the most prominent legacy and the city's most visited attraction – enough of old Bucharest remains to paint a picture of the city that was lost under the bulldozers of the 1980s. Art Deco apartment blocks and elegant Parisian-style villas line central streets, while the beautiful Orthodox churches of various eras provide respite from the bustle of the modern city. Bucharest's nightlife is sensational, and for many people it is the city's main selling point, flying in as they do from across Europe and the Middle East for hedonistic party weekends. Therme, Europe's most extensive thermal bath complex, just north of the city, has become a weekend destination in its own right.

PROMINENT ROMANIANS

It is perhaps fitting that Bucharest's finest house, on the city's most famous street, Calea Victoriei, once belonged to Romania's greatest musician and composer, George Enescu. A modest man, Enescu – who composed *Romanian Rhapsody* and taught Yehudi Menuhin to play the violin – preferred a far smaller building at the rear of the grand palace that now houses a museum to his life and work. Mircea Eliade, a philosopher (and in later life a professor at the University of Chicago) who was leading interpreter of religious experience, was born in Bucharest, but it is Romania's many sporting stars who have left a greater mark on the international arena. Footballer Gheorghe Hagi plied his trade at Bucharest clubs Sportul and Steaua before seeking fame at both Real Madrid and Barcelona; and Nadia Comaneci, although born in Onesti in northern Romania, trained in Bucharest before becoming the first gymnast to be awarded a perfect 10 at the Montreal Olympics in 1976. It is fitting that it was another Romanian, Lavinia Milosevic, who was awarded the last perfect 10 (in Barcelona in 1992) before the scoring system was changed. These days, it is tennis star Simona Halep who does Romania proud on the world stage – Bucharest bars and terraces fill up with fans watching her many Grand Slam finals.

FROZEN IN TIME

Romanian historian Lucian Boia, in his remarkable book *Romania: Borderland of Europe*, provides perhaps the quintessential description of contemporary Bucharest, whetting the appetite for long days pounding the streets in discovery of hidden gems. 'Bucharest is full of surprises,' he wrote in 2001. 'Nowhere – aside from the vast areas of blocks, where one block follows another – will you see two buildings the same. Not the same in style, in height, nor in size. And even the blocks can hide surprises: often you will find a whole street of old houses hidden behind a block, as if frozen in time.'

HISTORY AND CULTURE

There is no mention at all of a place called Bucharest until 1459, but no history of the city can begin there. The city's past is intertwined with the history of the Romanian people, who can trace their roots back more than 5,000 years to the Thracians, Dacians and – later – the Romans, who would eventually lend their name to Romania itself.

THRACIANS AND DACIANS

The first inhabitants of what is today Bucharest were almost certainly Paleolithic hunter-gatherers, although there is little hard evidence to back this up. Remarkable dwellings have been found at Ripiceni, near Botoşani in the far north Romania, and cave paintings at Cuciulat, in the county of Sălaj; both sites date from the upper Paleolithic age, around 10,000 BC, but both are some distance from Bucharest. There is then something of a historical void until the first evidence of Thracian tribes appearing in the region in the early Bronze Age, around 3000 BC. The Thracians were one of the original Indo-European tribes who populated vast swathes of Near-Asia and Europe. By 1000 BC there had been a delimitation of the Thracians into smaller, more homogenous tribes, of which the Getae and Dacians (usually known collectively as the Geto-Dacians, and from around 100 BC merely as Dacians) were two of the most important. Together they inhabited a vast area between the Danube and the Dniester, including the area in which present-day Bucharest sits.

By the beginning of the 7th century BC the Greeks had established several colonies along the Black Sea, including Tomis (present day Constanţa) and Callatis (Mangalia). Relations with the Dacians were usually good, and the area prospered. In 513 we get the first mention of the Dacians in written history: Herodutus tells us that during the expedition of Darius of Persia he was 'resisted in Dobrodgea by the Getae.' There is evidence (mainly coins found in the Tei lake on the outskirts of Bucharest) to suggest trade took place between a Geto-Dacian settlement close to present day Bucharest and the Greeks.

Old Court ruins.

THE ROMAN YEARS

Though the Scythians and Macedonians both made attempts to incorporate the Dacians into their empires, neither really succeeded, and by the time of Burebista, a Dacian king in the 1st century BC who united all Thracian tribes by fiercely resisting the Romans, we can talk of the existence of a genuine Dacian state. Greek historian Dionysopolis refers to Burebista as 'the first and most powerful of the kings who ever ruled Thrace'. Ruling from Sarmizegetusa, close to present day Craiova, about 400km (250 miles) west of Bucharest, Burebista was powerful enough to offer support to Pompey in his revolt against Julius Caesar, who, were it not for his murder, would have launched a full-scale invasion of Dacia.

It was Emperor Trajan, about to lead the Roman Empire to its zenith, who finally invaded Dacia, almost 150 years after Julius Caesar had died. The Roman victory was won in two campaigns (AD 101–2 and AD 105–6) fought against Decebal, usually remembered as the greatest Dacian king. In honour of his bravery, Trajan allowed him to commit suicide rather than be taken as a prisoner to Rome. Trajan's Column in Rome commemorates the Roman victory in the Dacian Wars. A full-size copy stands in Bucharest's History Museum.

The Romans did not stay long in Dacia. After the glorious period based on the virtue and abilities of Trajan, Hadrian and the two Antonines, the Empire went into decline and Dacia was one of the first provinces to be relinquished, abandoned to the Barbarians by Aurelian in 271. Evidence of how deeply Roman culture penetrated the native Dacian culture during the 165 years of occupation is today everywhere in Romania: the Romanian language, so close to Vulgar Latin, is the most obvious example.

SLAVS, MAGYARS AND THE AGE OF INVASION

After the retreat of the Romans the people left behind, these days known as Daco-Romans, were subjected to an innumerable number of invasions. First came the Goths, who had hounded the Romans out of much of northern and eastern Europe, then, in order, the Huns, Avars, Bulgars and Slavs all blazed a trail across what is today Romanian territory. The names of two Bucharest suburbs, Ilfov and Snagov, are Slav in origin, suggesting Slavic roots.

Magyars settled in Transylvania at the end of the 9th century, while the area of present-day Bucharest was at the time part of the First Bulgarian Empire, which it remained until around the beginning of the 11th century before succumbing to successive invasions of Pechenegs and Cumans.

The Mongols then briefly occupied the area before the Second Bulgarian Empire (which existed from around 1185 to 1396) swept them away. However, archaeological evidence suggests present-day Bucharest was uninhabited during much of the 12th and 13th centuries.

THE MIDDLE AGES: THE FORMATION & CONSOLIDATION OF THE PRINCIPALITIES

The legend claiming that Bucharest was founded by a shepherd, Bucur, only appeared in the 19th century and can probably be dismissed as nothing more than a myth. A more likely founding father is Black Radu (Radu Negru), the first ruler of the nascent principality of Wallachia, whose capital was at Curtea de Argeş.

Transylvania had emerged as a relatively modern, well-run feudal principality firmly within the Kingdom of Hungary by the end of the 13th century. Indeed, two great men of Transylvania, Iancu de Hunedoara, and his son, Matei Corvin, ruled Hungary for much of the 15th century. Matei Corvin (or King Mátyás as he is known in Hungary) is often cited as Hungary's greatest ever king.

To the south, a defeat of Hungary by the Wallachian prince, Basarab, at Posada in 1330, confirmed Wallachia as an independent principality. Basarab entered into pacts with Serb and Bulgar rulers to the east and south to consolidate his lands, and his son and successor, Nicolae Alexandru, obtained the recognition of Byzantium.

In Moldavia it was a similar story. After initial Hungarian domination of the area during the early 14th century, Prince Bogdan of Cuhea formalised Moldavian independence after a number of military victories against Hungarian forces during the winter of 1364–5. In both Wallachia and Moldavia independence brought brief but rich periods of church and monastery building, and often brutal implementation of the feudal system along western European lines.

VLAD THE IMPALER

It was Vlad III Dracula, also known as Vlad Țepeș (or Vlad the Impaler) – later to become the inspiration for Bram Stoker's *Dracula* – who put Bucharest on the map.

Even before the Ottoman sack of Constantinople in 1453, the Turks had been occupying vast swathes of Byzantine land in southeastern Europe. They first reached the Danube in 1395, but were defeated by Wallachian prince Mircea Cel Batran (Mircea the Old). Yet he could not hold out against the Ottomans forever, accepting Turkish domination in 1415 and agreeing to pay a yearly tribute to the Sublime Porte in exchange for relative independence. Moldavia, under the leadership of Alexandru Cel Bun (Alexander the Good) held out against Turkey for longer, but after his death in 1432 it too had to succumb to Ottoman rule.

After originally being a reliable ally of Turkey, Ştefan Cel Mare (Stephen the Great), Prince of Moldavia from 1457 to 1504 and often regarded as the greatest Romanian king, turned against the Ottoman Empire in the mid-1470s and led a 30-year campaign of fierce opposition to Ottoman rule. Vlad the Impaler led similar anti-Turk campaigns in Wallachia, having set up a court in what is now Bucharest's Old Town in the mid-1400s. It quickly became the preferred summer residence of Wallachian rulers, although the capital was by now at Târgoviște. Remnants of Bucharest's original Wallachian court (and its church) can be seen on Strada Franceza. In 1476, Bucharest was sacked twice: first by the Turks, and then by Stephen the Great. After Stephen died, in 1504, the Ottoman Empire further grew in size. In 1541 Hungary was wiped off the map of Europe. Wallachia, as well as Transylvania and Moldavia, became integral parts of the Ottoman Empire.

17TH AND 18TH CENTURIES

Though Mihai Bravu (Mihai the Brave) briefly united the three Romanian principalities for a short period in 1600, all three states remained firmly within the Ottoman sphere – while retaining certain independence – until the Turkish defeat at the Gates of Vienna in 1683 began the decline of the Sublime Porte's influence in Europe.

Transylvania was restored to Hungarian (now Habsburg) rule in 1687, while Moldavia and Wallachia became increasingly difficult for the Turks to control.

They responded by installing Greek Phanariots to rule in their stead, no longer trusting local princes. Though the Phanariots initially set about reforming the principalities, developing commerce, agriculture and the general administration, they quickly became appalling rulers, who heavily taxed the local noble

Mihae the Brave, Prince of Wallachia.

Queen Marie of Romania.

and peasant populations. Transylvania, meanwhile, under relatively enlightened Habsburg rule, prospered. Serfdom in the principality was abolished by Emperor Joszef in 1785.

19TH CENTURY: INDEPENDENCE

A peasant revolt in 1821 forced the Turks to restore the rule of native Romanian princes to the provinces of Wallachia and Moldavia. After the Russo-Turkish war of 1828–9 Wallachia and Moldavia became Russian protectorates, though officially remaining within the Ottoman Empire. Bucharest underwent a period of modernisation in the 1830s under the governorship of a Russian general, Pavel Kiseleff. So well are Kiseleff's reforms remembered that one of the city's most prominent boulevards is named for him.

In 1859, Prince Alexandru Ioan Cuza was elected as prince of both Wallachia and Moldavia. In 1861 the two principalities were united as Romania, which declared itself independent of Turkey in 1877. The new country was formally recognized at the Congress of Berlin in 1878, and in 1881 Prince Karl, of the House of Hohenzollern, was invited to become King Carol of Romania.

EARLY 20TH CENTURY: WORLD WAR I AND UNIFICATION

Romania remained neutral at the outbreak of World War I, the king's German ancestry countering the Romanian people's sympathy for the French. In 1916, however, Romania entered the war, seizing what it saw as an opportunity to wrest Transylvania from the clutches of the disintegrating Habsburg Empire. At war's end the negotiating skills of Nicolae Titulescu and the considerable charm of Queen Marie of Romania, granddaughter of Queen Victoria of England and wife of Ferdinand, who had succeeded Carol in 1916, saw Romania almost double in size. The three Romanian principalities were formally enjoined in 1919, with Bucharest as the capital.

BETWEEN THE WARS

Though life was good for some in the 1920s, especially among Bucharest's rich set, the country nevertheless remained backward for much of the decade. Poverty was widespread – unsurprising given that political stability was non-existent. King Carol II, who succeeded his father Ferdinand, was a poor leader whose attempts to constantly manipulate the political parties forbade any cohesive government from ever taking root. In 1938 Carol grew tired of the political parties altogether and declared a Royal dictatorship. He was forced to abdicate by the military in 1940, giving way to his young son Mihai, who in turn deferred almost all political decisions to an army general, Ion Antonescu.

WORLD WAR II

Caught between the Soviet devil and the Nazi deep blue sea, Romania tried desperately to stay out of World War II for as long as possible. Its hand was forced however, by the German decision to award Northern Transylvania to Horthyist Hungary, and by the Soviet Union's annexation of Bessarabia, the eastern part of Moldavia. Subtle German promises of Northern Transylvania's return, as well as British assurances of non-intervention, saw Romania join in Operation Barbarossa in 1941, invading Bessarabia side by side with the German army, and quickly retaking the territory it had lost. It was only when Antonescu committed Romanian troops to continuing into sovereign Soviet territory that the Allies declared war on Romania. Romania meantime, which had been enacting harsh anti-Semitic legislation since the 1930s, declared war on its Jews. It is estimated that between 271,000 and 286,000 Romanian Jews were murdered during World War II.

After the defeat of the Axis powers at Stalingrad, where tens of thousands of Romanians lost their lives, the end for Romania was swift. Antonescu was ousted by King Mihai in a palace coup on August 23rd 1944, and Romania rejoined the war on the side of the Allies three days later.

THE COMMUNIST TAKEOVER AND GHEORGHE GHEORGHIU-DEJ

The classic communist party 1-2-3 – of acting as a minority coalition partner, then a majority coalition partner, and finally as a one-party government – worked perfectly in Romania from 1944 to 1947, when the king was exiled, all other political parties were banned and the country was declared a people's republic. Red terror swept the country, with tens of thousands murdered or put to work in labour camps, including the most infamous at the Black Sea Canal.

Overseeing it all was the brutal Gheorghe Gheorghiu-Dej. Dej led a group of supporters who had remained in Romania during the war, and which by the late 1940s had defeated a group led by Ana Pauker, who had spent the war in Moscow. Dej was initially a strict disciple of Soviet policy, but by 1955 he had grown impatient with the Soviet Union's refusal to assist Romania in its quest to industrialise. Aided by the fact that Soviet troops were no longer stationed in Romania (the last member of the Red Army left in 1953), Dej was able to carve out a relatively independent path for Romania, and proceeded with rapid industrialisation. By the late 1950s the political terror had eased too.

Soviet (Russian) tanks in Romania, 1940.

1965–89: NICOLAE CEAUŞESCU

On Dej's death in 1965 the relatively young Nicolae Ceauşescu was appointed leader of the Communist Party. Ceauşescu, no intellectual, was nevertheless a clever political operator; by 1968 he had removed all of Dej's former associates from any positions of power. Later that year he memorably condemned the Soviet invasion of Czechoslovakia, a political masterstroke that cemented his power at home and secured him superstar status in Washington, Paris and London.

Buoyed by his popularity, Ceauşescu began a slow descent towards utter megalomania. The 1970s were marked by industrialisation on a huge scale and a sharp drop in living standards. In 1977, a massive earthquake hit Bucharest, killing more than 1,500. By the 1980s, when Ceauşescu began destroying much of the historic centre of the capital to construct a new Civic Centre fit for his 'New Socialist Man', he had clearly gone utterly mad.

THE REVOLUTION AND THE FALL OF CEAUŞESCU

By 1989 Romania was a failed country. It had a leader and a government, but little else. Schools closed early in winter for a lack of heating, nobody worked as people spent all day queuing for basic foodstuffs, and a rampant black market saw speculators and shadowy middle-men make small fortunes.

Yet even as late as November 1989, when the Communist Party held its four-yearly congress, electing Ceauşescu as president (unanimously, as usual) for another four-year term, there was no sign that the regime was in any trouble. As communist regimes crumbled all over Eastern Europe, Ceauşescu held on. Then came Timişoara.

Always better informed than the rest of the country (they could watch Yugoslav television), the population of Timişoara staged their first demonstration on December 15, initially in protest at the demotion of a local priest. The demonstrations became political and spread. Ceauşescu held a rally in Bucharest on 21 December to reassure the population that he was in control, but he wasn't. Despite much gunfire, demonstrators spent much of the evening of 21–22 December on Bucharest's streets, especially around Piaţa Universităţii. Ceauşescu and his wife Elena fled by helicopter from the roof of the Central Committee building (today the Ministry of the Interior) on the afternoon of the next day. Minutes later, demonstrators ransacked the building.

Inside, a new government had already been formed. Ion Iliescu, who until the early 1980s had been one of Ceauşescu's most loyal henchmen, led a group calling itself the National Salvation Front (FSN). It officially declared itself the new government on 23 December. On 25 December, Christmas Day, Ceauşescu and his wife – who had been captured on 23 December – were tried by a kangaroo court and shot in the town of Târgovişte. To this day it is not known if the shots fired at demonstrators throughout the revolution came from Ceauşescu loyalists or by forces loyal to the new regime, which – it has been suggested – needed martyrs to give itself credibility in the eyes of the general public. What is generally agreed however is that the FSN had been organised long before December 1989, perhaps as early as the previous winter.

ROMANIA SINCE 1989

Despite promising initially that the FSN would be a purely transitional government, the organization fielded candidates in the

The grave of communist dictator Nicolae Ceausescu.

elections of May 1990. Though allegedly free and fair, the FSN's absolute control of the media and all state apparatus meant that anything other than a resounding victory for FSN and Iliescu – who ran for president – was never in question. Soon after, in early June 1990, appalled at the apparent replacement of one authoritarian regime with another, students and workers in Bucharest demonstrated against the new regime, demanding that the FSN remove itself from politics and that Iliescu step down. The demonstration was brutally put down by miners, brought in by Iliescu to do the job the Securitate political police would have done in the communist days. More than 100 demonstrators died in what became known as the *Mineriadă*. Further demonstrations and a second *Mineriadă* in 1991 finally brought down the government, though Iliescu hung on, appointing a technocrat, Teodor Stolojan, to oversee the writing of a new constitution and to organise new elections. The latter too place in 1992; though better organised, the opposition was still soundly defeated. Iliescu remained president and his PSD (the renamed FSN) formed a new government that became a byword for theft, corruption and economic stagnation.

Iliescu was temporarily removed from power in 1996, only to be reelected in 2000, having changed the constitution in order to be able to run for a third term in office. Finally forced to step down in 2004, having been unable to change the constitution a second time, Iliescu's anointed successor, Adrian Nastase was easily defeated by the populist Traian Băsescu, erstwhile mayor of Bucharest. Băsescu served two terms, overseeing Romania's entry to the European Union in 2007.

Basescu was replaced by an ethnic German, Klaus Iohannis, in 2015. Throughout 2017 and 2018, large-scale demonstrations took place in Bucharest, with locals protesting against the government's failure to deal with corruption, which remains endemic; in 2018, the government brutally put down one such demonstration, leaving hundreds injured. Iohannis has seen attempts at further reform hampered by a PSD government, but was also deemed responsible for the political crisis of 2021, which almost brought down the coalition government; during his rule, Romania has steadily slid down the global indexes of democracy ("beating" Hungary to last place in the EU) and press freedom.

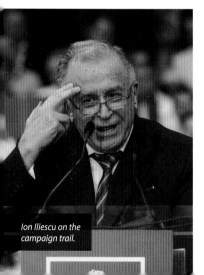

Ion Iliescu on the campaign trail.

HISTORICAL LANDMARKS

513 BC First recorded mention of the Geto-Dacians: the ancestors of the Romanians.

AD 106–271 Dacia, comprising much of present-day Romania, is part of the Roman Empire.

c.1300 The three Romanian principalities of Wallachia, Moldavia and Transylvania emerge from the Dark Ages as recognisable states.

1415 Wallachia accepts Ottoman rule.

1459 First mention of the city of Bucharest, as the summer court of Vlad the Impaler.

1541 Transylvania and Moldavia become part of the Ottoman Empire.

1687 Transylvania returned to Hungary.

1829 Wallachia becomes a Russian protectorate, although still part of the Ottoman Empire.

1877 As Romania, Wallachia and Moldavia declare independence from the Ottomans.

1919 Greater Romania forms from Transylvania, Wallachia and Moldavia.

1941 Romania enters World War II on the side of the Axis powers.

1944 On August 23 Romania leaves the war, only to reenter three days later on the side of the Allies.

1977 Major earthquake hits Bucharest, killing more than 1,500 people.

1989 Nicolae Ceaușescu is shot on Christmas Day after a popular revolution, in which 1,033 die.

2003 Romania is admitted to NATO.

2004 Former mayor of Bucharest Traian Băsescu elected Romanian president.

2007 Romania joins the EU.

2015 The Colectiv nightclub fire kills at least 26 people.

2018 Anti-government protests brutally put down by police.

2017 200,000-strong protest against government efforts to water down anti-corruption laws, the largest since the fall of communism.

2021 UEFA Euro Football Championships holds matches in Bucharest.

2021 Thousands of protesters gather to reject new Covid-19 restrictions.

2024 Major infrastructure work begins to improve driving conditions.

Bulevardul Unirii and the Palace of Parliament.

OUT AND ABOUT

While many of Bucharest's main sights are clustered around the city centre and can be reached on foot, a number of attractions may require the use of public transport. The city's metro system, as well as its many trams, buses and trolley-buses, serve most parts of the town; tickets are cheap.

For the most part, this section of the guide follows the natural layout of the city, starting in the Old Town – where Bucharest itself began – before exploring the new Civic Centre, the area built during the 1980s and which includes the country's most visited attraction, Parliament. It then follows the route of the town's most historic thoroughfare, Calea Victoriei, to the leafy northern part of the city, home to a number of good museums and parks. Then there is the Cotroceni district, home to Romania's president, as well as Cismigiu which brings us back to the city centre. We also provide details about excursions to the city's suburbs, and suggest a number of accessible day-trips further afield.

PIAȚA UNIVERSITĂȚII AND THE OLD TOWN

Bucharest lacks a real city centre, a focal point to which all roads lead. As such, a number of squares and piazzas have claims to be the city centre, though that of **Piața Universității** is the strongest. It was here that the 1989 revolution gathered strength, and where pitched battles were fought from behind barricades. In the centre of the square flowers and wooden crosses commemorate those who died here on the night of 21/22 December, 1989.

Southwest of Piața Universității is the area known as **Old Town**, or more commonly **Lipscani**, a street which runs through the centre of the district. This was the area in which Vlad Tepes created a

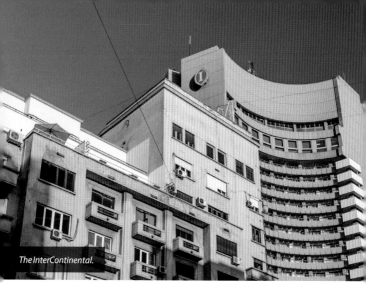
The InterContinental.

court in the 15th century; it subsequently became the site of plush city residences belonging to the Romanian elite, though fell into disrepair during the communist era. Now mostly pedestrianised, the area has undergone a vast amount of renovation, and has become a centre of the city's impressive nightlife scene.

PIAȚA UNIVERSITĂȚII

The tall **Grand** hotel ❶ just north of Piața Universității will be immediately recognisable to anyone who has seen footage of the Romanian Revolution of 1989, or the *Mineriadă* riots of 1990. From its balconies, journalists from around the world had a bird's eye view of events going on below. Built in the early 1970s as the *InterContinental*, it was the first modern hotel in the city and its lobby bar was a notorious listening post for the communist-era secret police, the Securitate. On the top floor is the country's highest swimming pool, complete with a sun terrace offering quite amazing views of the city centre, the Old Town area in particular. Although the hotel does not advertise the fact, if you just want to take the lift to the top in order to get some great shots of the city, nobody appears to mind.

Directly in front of the hotel is Romania's brutal-looking **National Theatre** ❷ (Teatrul Național). The original theatre was built between 1967 and 1970, and was rather abstractly styled to honour the architecture of Moldova's famous monasteries. In 1984 a grey, concrete, vaguely neoclassical casing was placed over the earlier structure, but this was removed in 2011 when the theatre began to take on its current shape – which is even uglier. The strange bronze statue in front of the theatre, called the **Caruta cu paiate**, is a tribute to Romania's best-loved playwright, Ion Luca Caragiale, and features characters from his plays.

Bucharest's **university** ❸ (universitate) stands to the west of Piața Universității, and gave the square gets its name. The building was constructed from 1857–69 at the request of Prince Alexandru Ioan Cuza, the first leader of a united Romania, but he had to flee into exile before the building was completed. Heavily damaged during Allied bombing in 1944, it was reconstructed during the 1950s but without many of its original Gothic flourishes.

On another corner of the square is the **Museum of Bucharest** ❹ (Muzeul

Caruta cu paiate.

Municipului București; www.muzeulbucurestiului.ro; Tue–Sun 10am–6pm), housed in the former Șuțu Palace, where costumes, photos and paintings depict life in Bucharest in the 18th and 19th centuries. Some of the original wooden panels that covered the surface of Calea Victoriei before it was paved have been preserved remarkably well and are on display. Opposite the museum is the enormous **Coltea Hospital** ❺ (Spitalul Coltea), the first to be built in the city, which dates back to 1704. In front of the hospital is the small but elegant **Coltea Church** (Biserica Coltea), dating from 1701.

MAGHERU

North of Piața Universității is **Bulevardul Magheru** ❻, named for a legendary Romanian World War I general. Lined with expensive shops, Art Deco apartment blocks, hotels, theatres and casinos, it is the closest that Bucharest comes to having a throbbing thoroughfare. It is also one of the busiest roads in Romania, and chock-full of traffic day and night. Look for the red-brick **Italian Church** ❼ (Biserica Italiana), with a neo-Gothic exterior, complete with Florentine tower, that is worth crossing to the other side of the street to admire.

Make sure you visit the small and often overlooked **Theodor Aman Museum** ❽ (Muzeul Theodor Aman, Strada C.A. Rosetti 8; www.muzeulbucurestiului.ro/muzeul-theodor-aman; Wed–Sun 10am–6pm), one of the most gorgeous and unique private houses in Bucharest. It was completed in 1868 to the artist Theodor Aman's own designs. Aman both lived and worked in the house, which has remained largely unchanged for 150 years: he donated it to the state on his death, and it has been a museum dedicated to his life and work since 1908. Besides showcasing a large number of Aman's paintings, the interior features murals that were mostly painted by Aman, and wood carvings made by German-born Romanian sculptor Karl Storck.

At the far end of Bulevardul Magheru is **Piaţa Româna ⓘ**, little more than a huge junction of several important arteries. The one building of interest is the **Economics University** (ASE) on the northwestern side.

OLD TOWN

There are many ways to access Bucharest's Old Town, but the most spectacular is via **Strada Toma Caragiu**, opposite the university. Caragiu was one of

Bulevardul Magheru.

Romania's best-loved actors before being killed in the 1977 earthquake. The street is flanked by two once identical 19th-century neoclassical buildings, although the eastern building has lost many of its original elements due to renovations. At the southern end of the street is the so-called **Russian Church ⓘ** (Biserica Sf. Nicolae), which gets its name not only from its distinctive Russian-style onion domes, but also from the fact that it was financed by a gift of 600,000 golden roubles from then Russian Tsar Nicholas II. Completed in 1909, the gilded iconostasis is reputedly a copy of that in Archangelsk Monastery in Moscow's Kremlin, but the interior – unusually for Orthodox churches – also includes a number of floral, Art Nouveau flourishes.

Moving deeper into the Lipscani area the impressive **Romanian National Bank ⓘ** (Banca Naţionala a României; Mon–Fri 10am–5pm), is a neoclassical gem dating from 1885. The main banking hall is outstandingly preserved, and guided tours offer a fascinating insight into Romanian monetary, banking and cultural history. You will also see the oldest coins ever minted in Romania. To join a tour you will need to reserve a place a day in advance; photo ID is required.

A short walk from here along Strada Stavropoleos is the **Stavropoleos Monastery** ⓬ (Mănăstirea Stavropoleos), with a church that is one of the smallest and yet most strikingly beautiful in Bucharest. It was completed in 1724 and features beautiful stone and wood carvings, particularly on the main doors. The courtyard colonnades – most pleasant on hot summer days – house a significant collection of finely engraved tombstones, and if you are lucky you might see skilled craftsmen at work restoring them. Just opposite is the city's most famous restaurant, **Caru cu bere** ⓭ (see page 103), with an ornate interior, complete with wood carvings and painted ceilings, that is worth a look even if you have no desire to eat here.

Back on Strada Lipscani is **Hanul cu Tei** ⓮, a superb covered alleyway – once a *han*, or inn – where you can pick up excellent value arts, crafts and antiques in the small shops and workshops. Note that most shops close early on Saturday and do not open at all on Sunday. Strada Lipscani itself was long known for its fabric shops and gets its name from the Liepzig traders who used to sell their wares here in the 18th century. Like many of the cobbled pedestrian streets of the Old Town (notably stradas Smardan, Gabroveni, Selari and Covaci) Lipscani has over the past decade become a hub of **Bucharest nightlife**. Bars, pubs, restaurants and clubs line the various streets, and during the summer all have large terraces, which can make navigating the area something of an obstacle course.

At the southern end of the Old Town is another old inn, the **Hanul lui Manuc** ⓯ (see page 104), a world-famous *caravanserai* where traders and horsemen would eat and drink while horses rested in the stables below. Many of the original features remain, including the splendid entrance and courtyard. These days it's a popular restaurant, which brews its own excellent beer and offers a shady place to while away long, lazy afternoons and evenings. The inn is popular for weddings, and if you come here on just about any Saturday or Sunday in the summer you are likely to see a Romanian wedding party in full flow. Opposite is the Byzantine-style **Old Court Church** ⑯ (Biserica Curtea Veche). Built as long ago as 1559, it is the oldest church in Bucharest, and the astonishing frescoes inside are original. In front are the ruins of the **Old Court** (Curtea Veche) itself, where Vlad Țepeș established a summer court in the 15th century. The Old Court is occasionally used to host exhibitions.

There is a smaller pedestrianised area of old houses and buildings on the other side of Bulevardul I.C. Bratianu (you can traverse

Stavropoleos Monastery.

Hanul lui Manuc.

the roadway via an underpass). You should not miss the superb
New St George's Church ⑰ (Biserica Sf. Gheorghe Nou), although
it is hardly new. Built, in fact, in 1699, it stands in the middle of Piaţa
Sf. Vineri, the point from where distances to and from Bucharest
are measured. In the church courtyard, a sundial shows the distance to many towns and cities across Romania. Note that one
of them is Chişinau, today in the Republic of Moldova but once
part of Romania. Besides its colourful and well-preserved frescoes
depicting a number of biblical scenes and the portraits of numerous Romanian saints, New St George's Church is the burial place
of Constantin Brâncoveanu, a Romanian prince killed by the Turks
after defying their orders to fight with them in the first Russo-
Turkish War. In 1830 the church was the site of Bucharest's first ever
Romanian-language bookshop.

Just to the south, and with its bell tower poking into Bulevardul
Bratianu, is the Roman-Catholic **Baraţiei Church** ⑱, built in 1828.

Boasting a couple of lovely stained-glass windows, the church holds services in Romanian and Hungarian. The current bell, which dates from 1855, was a gift from Habsburg Emperor Franz Josef. The name of the church, *Baraţiei*, derives from the Hungarian word for friend, *barat*.

THE CIVIC CENTRE

Few experiments in urban planning have gone so dreadfully wrong as that which saw vast areas of old Bucharest destroyed and rebuilt to the grandiose vision of megalomaniac dictator Nicolae Ceauşescu in the 1980s. **Piaţa Unirii**, the heart of what became known as the **Civic Centre** (Centru Civic), had for centuries been the soul of Bucharest, home to a busy daily market. Many locals will insist that the city lost any trace of that soul when the

KING CAROL

When Romania declared its independence from Turkey in 1877 its parliamentarians swept Europe in its search for a foreign monarch (local princes were infamous for infighting and deemed unsuitable). Karl Hohenzollern, a German prince, was volunteered for the job by Bismarck, no less, who though the presence of a Prussian king would assure Germany great influence in South Eastern Europe. He was wrong. Karl (who became Carol I of Romania) devoted himself to his new subjects, and was unswerving in his pursuit of an independent foreign policy. Even at the outbreak of World War I in 1914 he refused to side with Germany. He died in 1916, having reigned for almost 40 years, in which Romania was at peace for almost the whole time. His legacy includes the splendid palace he built in Sinaia: Peleş Castle.

*Aerial view of
Piața Universității.*

charming old square, and more than 20,000 houses and 70 churches around it, were destroyed and replaced with hastily-built apartment blocks and endless expanses of concrete. Hospitals, schools and even an Art Deco stadium built in the 1920s (remnants of whose terracing can still be seen on Strada Izvor, opposite the Ibis hotel) were also destroyed.

Three metro lines serve Piața Unirii, but for those in a hurry to visit Parliament, Izvor metro station is closest.

PIAȚA UNIRII

Today's **Piața Unirii** ⑲, is one of the world's largest public squares and a busy transport hub: three of the city's five metro lines intersect here, and all of Bucharest's night bus routes depart from the square. It is largely, alas, given over to traffic, but at its centre is a small park complete with a set of **ornamental fountains**, the focal point of a spectacular music, water and light show that takes place at 9.30pm every Friday evening during the summer.

On the eastern side of the square, the massive **Unirea Department Store** (Magazinul Unirea), built in the early 1970s, was the first modern shopping centre to open in the city.

The **Dâmbovița river**, which once flowed through the square, was hidden underground as part of the rebuilding of the 1980s, when Bucharest was almost entirely a construction site.

PALACE OF PARLIAMENT

There can be no building in the world as soulless as the **Palace of Parliament**  (Palatul Parlamentului; daily 10am–4pm; guided tours only), which dominates the Civic Centre and can be seen from most parts of Bucharest. Still often referred to by locals under its original name, Casa Poporului (the House of the People), it is found at the far end of **Bulevardul Unirii**, a wide street today lined with increasingly shabby neoclassical apartment blocks but originally built as a showpiece residential street of the new communist Romania (its original name was the Boulevard of Socialist Victory).

Built on one of the city's few hills, and on the site of the Mihai Voda Monastery (which was destroyed to make way for the palace; even the hill was levelled slightly), the parliament building is shrouded in mystery and legend to this day, and there are more myths surrounding it than any other building in the country (one claims that a secret metro line runs from under the building to Piaţa Unirii).

What is known for certain is that it is the largest palace in the world (excluding factories, it's almost the largest building full stop by volume), was built from 1984–90, has more than 3,500 rooms, and stands 84m (276ft) high; its total estimated cost topped $4 billion, although officially, it has never been finished.

Dam over the Dambovita river.

The building is Romania's most visited attraction, and was constructed using only indigenous materials, including the marble. Unless you are on official business, the only way to see the building is on one of the informative guided tours, the highlight of which is the main central balcony, from where you will get what is perhaps the defining view of communist-era Bucharest, along Bulevardul Unirii and out towards the rest of the Civic Centre: Piața Unirii and Piața Alba Iulia. The tour also takes in the **Sala Unirii** (Unification Hall) whose 14-ton carpet had to be woven on the premises by machinery specially made for the purpose. The room's **chandelier** makes use of 7,000 light bulbs.

Besides housing Romania's parliament (both the upper and lower chambers), the palace is also home to the **Romanian Museum of Contemporary Art ㉑** (Muzeul National de Arta

Marble staircase in the
Palace of Parliament.

Contemporana; Wed–Sun 10am–6pm). The museum makes superb use of the building's vast spaces and its permanent collection offers a quirky look at Romanian art from 1947 to the present day, offering a valuable insight into some of the subtle ways in which artists used their work to fight against the communist regime. The museum also has a rooftop café with impressive views of the city. Note that whether

Romanian Museum of Contemporary Art.

taking the guided tour of parliament or visiting the museum, you should bring photo ID and expect airport-level security checks. The entrance to both the palace tour and the museum are on the northern side of the building, facing Izvor Park.

PATRIARCHAL HILL

Patriarchal Hill ㉒ (Dealul Mitropoliei), which climbs from the southwestern corner of Piaţa Unirii is the seat of Daniel, head of the Romanian Orthodox Church. The walk up from Piaţa Unirii is lovely: look for the statues of Romanian legends Serban Cantacuzino and Alexandru Ioan Cuza.

At the top of the hill is a **bell tower**, built in 1698 during the reign of Constantin Brancoveanu as an entrance to a monastery – founded in 1650 – which once occupied the site. Beyond the tower is the centrepiece of the complex, a **church** (7am–8pm) which since 1925 has served as the Romanian Patriarchal Cathedral

Inside the Antim Monastery.

(and which will continue to do so until the new cathedral, see box, is complete). Built from 1656–8, the church is dedicated to Sts Constantin and Elena. It is considered a classic of what is known as Brâncovean design: many churches in Bucharest and around Romania look similar. Alas, with the exception of the icons representing Constantin and Elena (miraculously preserved, claim the faithful) the original frescoes – both interior and exterior – have all been destroyed. The current interior artwork was painted from 1932–5 in neo-Byzantine style, and is no less stunning than the original. The paintings of the 12 apostles which decorate the facade above the main entrance are even more recent, added during significant restoration of the church in 2008.

Inside, a splendid chandelier competes with the golden altar for attention. The cathedral also houses (in a glorious silver case) the remains of St Dumitru – the patron saint of Bucharest, brought here in 1774 – as well as relics of Constantin and Elena. On both

May 21 (Sts Constantin and Elena) and October 26 (St Dumitru) the queues of worshippers standing patiently in line to enter the church lead back down the hill as far as Piața Unirii and beyond. The church boasts one of the finest acapella choirs in the country and its call to prayer is well worth waking early to hear.

Surrounding the church are two buildings of equal historical importance. To the right is the modest yet elegant construction which serves as the home and private chapel of the patriarch. Originally built at the same time as the church opposite, it served as the residence of the monastery's abbot before being extended twice – in 1723 and 1932 – to accommodate the patriarch's apartments.

On the other side of the square is the far larger **Patriarchal Palace**, which has on a couple of occasions served a political purpose. Constructed between 1903 and 1907 the building's cupola – which collapsed during an earthquake in 1940 before being rebuilt – is styled on that of the Ateneul Român (see page 53). The building was originally the home of Romania's Chamber of

THE CATHEDRAL OF NATIONAL SALVATION

Behind the Palace of Parliament a new building just as epic in proportions is slowly taking shape: the **Cathedral of National Salvation** (Catedrala Mantuirii Neamului). Construction on what will be the largest church in Eastern Europe has been underway for several years, and despite being consecrated in 2018, completion is not scheduled until at least 2025. The vast cost of the project, much of which has been met by public funds, has been criticised by civil society groups. The cathedral's bell, engraved with a portrait of Daniel, the current Romanian patriarch, is the world's largest free-swinging church bell, weighing over 25 tons.

Deputies, and was put to use in the immediate aftermath of the 1989 revolution as the location of Romania's first post-communist, democratic parliament.

THE HIDDEN MONASTERIES

Another church and monastery, the **Antim Monastery ㉓**, is just west of Mitropoliei, completely hidden behind high-rise apartment blocks. One of the monastery's buildings was in fact moved 20m/yds (on rails) to make way for the apartments (a number of churches around Bucharest were saved from the bulldozers in this way). The church, which dates from 1812, is topped with splendid eastern-style domes, in coruscating gold, while inside the original **icon of the nativity** is equally stunning.

Southeast of Piața Unirii, again hidden behind apartment blocks (Ceaușescu never sought to completely destroy the Orthodox Church, as he needed it from time to time to lend legitimacy to his regime, but he did want to hide it from public view) is the walled 16th-century **Radu Voda Monastery ㉔**, with well-kept grounds. The original monastery church was built in 1508, although the current structure mainly dates from 1613–4. Extensive renovation was carried out during the 19th century, when the stunning frescoes (all the work of artist Gheorghe Tattarescu) were added. Justinian, a controversial patriarch of the Romanian Orthodox Church during the 1950s and '60s, often accused of collaborating with the communist regime, is buried in the grounds. The inscription on his headstone reads: 'I fought the good fight. I guarded the faith.'

Directly opposite the monastery is the tiny **Bucur Church ㉕**, said to be Bucharest's oldest. It has been consolidated in order to prevent it falling further towards the Dâmbovița river, just a few metres to the rear. The church is named for Bucur the Shepherd, the mythological founder of the Romanian capital.

OLD JEWISH DISTRICT

Almost all of Bucharest's Jewish district, including a number of synagogues, was destroyed during the demolitions of the 1980s to make way for the Civic Centre. The area was centred on the **Choral Temple** ㉖ (Templul Coral) behind **Piaţa Unirii**, first built in 1857, then rebuilt in 1866 following its destruction in a pogrom. It is a replica of Vienna's Leopoldstadt-Tempelgasse Great Synagogue and features a lavishly decorated two-level interior. It remains a working synagogue, serving Bucharest's dwindling yet active Jewish community.

There are two other synagogues close by. The **Great Synagogue** ㉗ (Sinagoga Mare; Sun–Thu 8.30am–2.30pm, Fri 8.30am–12.30pm) houses a small but moving exhibition devoted to the Holocaust in Romania, while the **Holy Union Temple** ㉘ (Templul

Radu Voda Monastery.

The National Library.

Unirea Sfântă; Mon–Thu 10am–5pm, Sun 9am–12.30pm) hosts a far larger exhibition devoted to Jewish history in Romania. Its collection celebrates Jewish Romanian family life at home, in the community and in the synagogue.

On the other side of the Old Town on the banks of the Damobovita river is a **Holocaust Memorial** ❷⓿ erected in 2009, which has a small hall of remembrance (open around the clock) and a number of plaques on which are engraved the names of many of the victims of the Holocaust in Romania.

ALONG CALEA VICTORIEI

Calea Victoriei is Bucharest's most celebrated and historic street. It has had many names over the years, including Ulița Sarindar, Drumul Brașovului and Drumul Mogoșoaia – its name until 1878 when it was christened Calea Victoriei in honour of victories recently won by Romanian armies fighting to preserve the country's newly won independence from the Ottoman Empire. More than 3km (1.8 miles) in length, it meanders its way from the Dâmboviţa river in the south to Piaţa Victoriei in the north, passing through the city centre along the way. It is lined with a number of significant historic buildings, hotels, museums and attractions, and we recommend finding the time to walk its entire length, from south to north. To do so is to take a lesson in Romanian history, art and architecture.

FROM THE RIVER TO PIAŢA REVOLUŢIEI

Climbing briefly uphill, with the Old Town to the east, stop at the **National History Museum** ㉚ (Muzeul Naţional de Istorie; www. mnir.ro; Wed–Sun 10am–5pm). The best sections are those relating to the Roman period, including a cast of Trajan's Column in Rome.

THE HOLOCAUST

Romania began passing anti-Jewish legislation in the late 1930s, and in 1941 there were violent pogroms in Bucharest and the northern city of Iaşi. Deportations to Transnistria in present-day Moldova followed, and while many Romanian Jews survived World War II (particularly those in the south of the country), Romania was responsible for the deaths of more Jews than any country other than Germany itself. According to the official Wiesel Commission report, released by the Romanian government in 2004, Romania killed a total of between 271,000 and 286,000 Jews during World War II. On the west side of the Old Town, on the bank of the Damobovita river, the **Holocaust Memorial** has a small hall of remembrance, and a number of plaques on which are engraved the names of many local victims of the Holocaust.

The Romanian Treasury includes jewellery from the time of the Geto-Dacians, as well as the current Romanian Crown Jewels: the king's crown and an amazing selection of emerald jewellery made for Queen Marie, wife of Romanian King Ferdinand and grand-daughter of Queen Victoria. The museum building itself is fabulous, constructed from 1894–1900 to the designs of local architect Alexandru Săvulescu. It originally served as the headquarters of the Romanian postal service. The somewhat strange statue on the museum's steps represents Emperor Trajan holding a wolf.

On the other side of the street to the museum is **CEC** ③① (Casa de Economii si Consemnațiuni), the headquarters of the national savings bank. Its fabulous façade, not least the huge arch covering the entrance, is one of the city's best. The interior is equally impressive, boasting elaborate murals and a stunning glass roof, and a dome that suggests the style of later Byzantine-era churches. Opposite is the **Zlatari Church**, built in the 1850s and most notable for its interior frescoes.

A small public square sits in front of Romania's **Military Club** ③② (Cercul Militar), built in 1912 on the site of a former Sarindar monastery (the memory of which is preserved in the name of the fountain directly in front of the building). Most of the building is

PASAJUL MACCA-VILLACROSSE

The glass-ceilinged **Macca-Villacrosse Passage** (Pasajul Macca-Villacrosse) was built at the end of the 19th century to link Calea Victoriei with the Romanian National Bank (see page 35). It is named for a Catalan architect, Xavier Villacrosse, who from 1840–50 was the chief architect of Bucharest. Bursting with natural light, it was originally home to jewellery shops, but today a large number of cafés and bars make use of its commercial spaces.

only open to those on military business. Opposite, the historic **Casa Capsa** hotel and restaurant ❸ was the preferred meeting place of Bucharest's literary set in the 1920s and 1930s.

Following the curve of the road and passing the **Odeon Theatre** (opened in 1911, and today guarded by a statue of the great Turkish leader Kemal Ataturk), the modern **Novotel** hotel stands on the site of Romania's original National Theatre, destroyed in an Allied bombing raid in 1944. The entrance is an exact replica of that of the theatre.

Macca-Villacrosse Passage.

PIAŢA REVOLUŢIEI

It was at **Piaţa Revoluţiei** ❸ that Romania's communist regime finally came to an end in December 1989, when Nicolae Ceauşescu fled from the roof of what was then the Communist Party Central Committee Building, just as demonstrators broke in. Today the building houses the Romanian **Ministry of the Interior**, and the balcony from which Ceauşescu made his final address is pointed out – literally, via means of a well-placed crack – by a small memorial to the revolution. A larger monument to the revolution towers rather awkwardly above the square; locals have nicknamed it 'the olive on a cocktail stick'.

South of the square is the **Creţulescu Church** (Biserica Creţulescu), fully restored after being badly damaged during the

revolution. It was built in the 1720s, and the outstanding paintings on the entrance are original, the work of an unknown artist.
The bust in front of the church is of Corneliu Coposu, a liberal
Romanian politician of the 1940s who was imprisoned by the com-
munists for decades in appalling conditions.

Next to the church is Romania's former Royal Palace, today the
National Museum of Art (Muzeul Național de Arta; www.mnar.
ro; Wed–Sun 11am–6pm, until 7pm May–Sept). The building was
completed in 1812 by a wealthy landowner, but became state
property in 1859 when his sons squandered away their inheritance
and ran up huge debts. It was then the residence of Romania's royal
family until 1947, when its last resident, King Mihai, fled into exile.
Today the country's premier art gallery, it houses works by all of
Romania's greatest painters, including Nicolae Grigorescu, Theodor

Hotel Novotel.

Aman and Gheorghe Tatarescu. It also has a vast collection of European Old Masters and an entire floor devoted to Romanian religious art, including icons, carved altars, illustrated manuscripts and bibles, and fragments of frescoes from the country's monasteries. The restored former royal living quarters and throne room can be seen on guided tours held on occasional weekends.

Piața Revolutiei's northern side is dominated by the **InterContinental Athénée Palace** . Besides being the most luxurious hotel in the city, it is a living piece of Bucharest's history. It was built in 1912, and during World War II it saw much intrigue and scheming – it was reportedly was the site of secret negotiations between the Nazis and the Allies, and figures prominently in Olivia Manning's *The Balkan Trilogy*. Its terrace, on Calea Victoriei, is the swankiest in town. The more modern **Radisson Blu** stands opposite, and boasts one of the city's few outdoor pools.

In front of the Hilton is the remarkable **Ateneul Român** (Roman Atheneum; www.fge.org.ro), a stunning late 19th-century neoclassical concert hall, today the home of the Romanian Philharmonic Orchestra. The interior can only be seen by attending a concert, but they are held most evenings, and it is so glorious that it is worth buying a ticket (they are cheap) even if you have no interest in classical music.

TOWARDS PIAȚA VICTORIEI

North from the *InterContinental*, Calea Victoriei narrows and becomes more residential, but there remain a number of fine houses and churches to be admired. In a small square on the corner of Strada George Enescuis the **White Church** ❸ (Biserica Alba, Biserica Sf. Nicolae) is one of the oldest in Bucharest, founded in 1700. The current building dates from 1827, however, as the original was destroyed in an earthquake. The interior frescoes for which it is famed have been restored a number of times, most recently in 1988.

Athénée Palace Hilton.

Further along is the Romanit Palace, which houses the **Museum of Art Collections** ㊱ (Muzeul Colecţiilor de Artă; www.mnar.arts. ro; Wed–Sun 10am–6pm). The palace was built in 1834, and for much of the 19th century was home to the Ministry of Finance, becoming an art museum in 1948. It displays the collections of some of Romania's wealthiest families and includes a rich selection of Romanian art, as well as pieces brought from Asia and Africa. The lower ground floor is home to a fine collection of statuary going back as far as the 15th century.

The mansion a short distance further along is the **Casa Vernescu** (www.palacecasinobucharest.ro; over 18s only), built in 1820 and long regarded as the finest house in the city. The building is now home to a casino and restaurant, and it is worth taking a look inside at the ornate decor.

At Calea Victoriei 141 is the former home of George Enescu, today the **George Enescu Museum** ㊲ (Muzeul George Enescu;

www.georgeenescu.ro; Tue–Sun 10am–5pm) dedicated to this finest of Romania's composers. Its Art Nouveau entrance is gorgeous, but it is worth noting that Enescu, a modest man, apparently preferred to spend most of his time in the smaller building at the rear of the courtyard. The museum was closed at the time of writing, with no set date of completion.

AVIATORILOR AND HERĂSTRĂU PARK

Calea Victoriei emerges at **Piaţa Victoriei**, the gateway to northern Bucharest, far leafier and wealthier than the centre of the city, with noticeably fewer communist-era apartment blocks. The area is home to the city's finest and largest park, **Herăstrău**, packed with attractions.

THE MUSEUMS OF PIAŢA VICTORIEI

Piaţa Victoriei itself is another of Bucharest's many large public squares which at first glance can appear to be little more than a vast mass of tower blocks, concrete and traffic. In recent years it has become the preferred location for anti-government protests,

GEORGE ENESCU

The Romanian composer George Enescu (1881–1955) was a giant of modern music. Prodigiously gifted, he became best known in America as a conductor and in Europe as one of the greatest violinists of the 20th century (and indeed he taught the great Yehudi Menuhin). Yet he was first and foremost a composer; though the majority of his works, including the sublime Romanian Rhapsody, remain little known outside of Romania. Every two years, an international classical music festival is held in Bucharest in his honour.

for on the eastern side is the **Victoria Palace** (Palatul Victoriei), since 1990 the seat of the Romanian government. An elegant, linear construction with a marble facade that apes the neoclassical architecture popular in Italy at the time, it was completed in 1937 and originally housed the country's Foreign Ministry. It is closed to all but those on official business.

Opposite is the **Peasant Museum** ❸❽ (Muzeul Național al Țăranului Român; www.muzeultaranuluiroman.ro; Tue–Sun 10am–6pm). One of the city's best museums, it is packed with well-presented exhibits that tell the fascinating story of the extraordinary survival and inventiveness of the Romanian peasant. It's an immersive experience, featuring log houses, windmills and a barn. There's a small but superb exhibition dedicated to communist iconography, and this is the one place in Romania where you will

George Enescu Museum.

see a bust of Vladimir Lenin. The museum also has probably the best souvenir shop in Romania, where only the finest handmade goods are sold, including delicately embroidered blouses, intricately painted Easter eggs and wood carvings. In the courtyard – which hosts craft fairs most weekends – is an original wooden church, brought to the museum in the 1990s from the Maramureș region in the far northwest of Romania.

The Peasant Museum.

Directly opposite the Peasant Museum is the less impressive **Geology Museum** (Muzeul Național al Geologiei; www.geology. ro; daily 10am–6pm), which does have a fine collection of fossils, rocks and minerals, but the museum building itself is in need of renovation.

Across the street, completing a trio of Piața Victoriei museums, is the **Grigore Antipa Natural History Museum** ❸ (www.antipa. ro; Apr–Oct Tue–Sun 10am–8pm, Nov–Mar Tue–Fri 10am–6pm, Sat–Sun 10am–7pm). It is home to a superb collection of exhibits, including Jurassic-era skeletons, but the finest part of the museum is the basement, where the displays provide an invaluable guide to the incredibly rich world of animal and plant life native to Romania. Children especially will love the many hands-on exhibits, experiments and films, and during the week the place is full of school groups. The life-sized giraffe standing in front of the entrance to the museum is a popular meeting point for locals.

Aviatorilor Monument.

TOWARDS HERĂSTRĂU

A long but rewarding walk the length of **Şoseaua Kiseleff** will take you past the well-kept Kiseleff Park, where tall trees provide welcome shade on hot summer days, and some of the largest and finest homes in Bucharest, these days mostly used as embassies or the headquarters of banks. The 20m (66ft) -high **Aviatorilor Monument** in the centre of the street was built in the late 1930s in honour of Romania's many aviation pioneers (one, Henri Coanda, for whom Bucharest's airport is named, invented an early form of the jet engine).

Somewhat incredibly, the body of the statue topping the monument was based on that of American boxer Joe Louis, who visited Bucharest at the time of its construction. In 1981 a replica of the monument was taken into space by Dumitru Prunariu, the first Romanian to go into orbit.

It is worth taking a slight detour east along Strada Paris to visit the **National Museum of Maps and Old Books** ⑩ (Muzeul Naţional al Hărţilor şi Cărţii Vechi; www.muzeulhartilor.ro; Wed–Sun 10am–6pm) housed in a beautiful 1920s villa, where the amazing collection consists of over 1,000 works dating back to the 16th century. The maps are impeccably presented and graphically tell a very clear story of how the three principalities that make up modern Romania developed over the centuries. The ceilings have been decorated with scenes from world mythology and astronomical maps, and the stained glass windows were designed with various heraldic emblems.

There is another excellent museum north of here on plush Bulevardul Primaverii (the most expensive property on the Bucharest version of the Monopoly board). Called the **Museum of Recent Art** ⓐ (Muzeul de Arta Recenta; www.mare.ro; daily 11am–7pm) it is set over five levels. The ground floor has a great café, Beans & Dots (see page 106) and the permanent exhibition includes a full retrospective of Romanian contemporary art from the 1960s to the present day. It is particularly insightful when dealing with the various risks and compromises artists were forced to make in order to break away from socialist realism. Guided tours are available.

A lavish bathroom in the Spring Palace.

THE SPRING PALACE

Contrary to popular belief, the Palace of Parliament (see page 41) never served (and was never intended to serve) as the residence of Nicolae Ceauşescu. Instead, the dictator lived with his wife and family in what was then called the Spring Palace, but is now referred to as **The House of Ceauşescu** ⓦ (Casa Ceauşescu; www.casaceausescu.ro; Tues–Sun 10am–5pm). Elegant from the outside, and with a splendid courtyard and garden, the interior betrays the kitsch tastes of Ceauşescu's wife, Elena. The building has its own cinema and swimming pool, and the taps were made of solid gold. The only way to see the building is to book a place on a guided tour, and you will need to do so at least one day in advance.

HERĂSTRĂU PARK

Although officially, since 2018, named **King Mihai I Park** ⓫ (Parcul Regele Mihai I al României), the vast majority of Bucharest's residents continue to refer to the city's largest park by its original name, **Herăstrău** (although for a short period in the 1950s it was known as Stalin Park). Spread over more than 187 hectares (462 acres) around Lake Herăstrău, it is one of the jewels in Bucharest's crown, and is incredibly popular with locals, especially on summer weekends when it can feel as though half the city has decided to visit. The park was created in the 1930s on what had until then been mainly marshland around the lake. During the late 19th century, however, parts of the lakeshore served as a promenade for Bucharest's wealthy, and the area surrounding the lake had long since become the most fashionable in the city. The official residence of Romania's royal family, the Elisabeta Palace (closed to the public), is inside the park.

There are various places at which you can access Herăstrău, but the main entrance is at **Piaţa Charles de Gaulle**, complete with a rather bizarre bronze statue of the former French president, once voted the ugliest statue in the city. There are a number of other statues around the park, mainly honouring Romania's best-loved writers and artists, including Nicolae Grigorescu, Constantin Brancuşi, Theodor Aman and Mihai Eminescu. There's even a memorial to Michael Jackson. There are boat trips on the lake during the summer months, and the cycling track surrounding the lake is very popular. Bikes are available to rent at the park's main entrance. A Japanese Garden features some of the most beautiful plants in the park, such as cherry blossoms and red Japanese maple. Lawns offer a choice of picnic spots, and there is a vast array of terraces, bars, cafés and restaurants. Those on the northern side of the lake tend to be upmarket and expensive, and those on the southern side more reasonably priced.

Herăstrău Park.

THE VILLAGE MUSEUM

Bucharest's **Arc de Triumf** ⓭ (viewing level: 10am–4pm) was first built, of wood, in 1919 to honour the country's World War I dead. The stone structure dates from 1927, and offers fabulous views of the northern part of the city from its viewing deck. The arch is the focal point of Romania's National Day celebrations, which take place on 1 December, during which a military parade passes through the arch while air force jets fly overhead.

A short walk north from the arch, alongside the edge of Herăstrău Park, will bring you to the **Village Museum** ⓯ (Muzeul Satului; https://muzeul-satului.ro/en; Tue–Sun 9am–5pm), a collection of original houses, wooden churches and other buildings from the Romanian countryside, brought to Bucharest by Royal Decree in 1936. Each of the buildings has a plaque showing exactly where in Romania it was previously located. Most of the houses date from end of the 19th century, but some are much earlier, such as those from Berbeşti, in the heart of Romania. The most-visited site in the museum is the steep belfry of the wooden Maramureş church, complete with faded icons. It is still a working church, and services are held here on Sundays and religious holidays. Also look for the earth houses of Straja, dug into the ground and topped with thatched roofs, and the colourful dwellings of the Danube Delta.

At the head of Soseaua Kiseleff is the monstrous **Free Press House** (Casa Presei Libere), built in the early 1950s and modelled on the Palace of Science and Culture in Warsaw, Poland (although the Bucharest version is much smaller). It houses the editorial offices of a number of Romanian newspapers, and the country's national archive.

A short walk north of the Free Press House is the **Nicolae Minovici Museum of Folk Art** ⓰ (Muzeul Nicolae Minovici; www.muzeulbucurestiului.ro/en/nicolae-minovici-folk-art-museum; Wed–Sun 10am–6pm), housed in a neo-Romanian style house built in 1906, surrounded by impressive landscaped gardens. Minovici, a doctor, founded Bucharest's first emergency hospital and spent his spare time travelling the country assembling a fine collection of traditional art and crafts, especially ceramics and woven fabrics. He bequeathed both his house and art collection to the city on his death in 1941.

Free Press House.

COTROCENI TO CISMIGIU

Often overlooked by visitors but with wide streets lined with linden trees and a mix of architecture including Art Deco, Cubist and more traditional Romanian styles, **Cotroceni** is an elegant neighbourhood, west of the Civic Centre, that is home to, among others, Romania's president.

THE PRESIDENTIAL PALACE

Romania's president has, since 1990, lived in the splendid **Cotroceni Palace and Museum** ⑰ (www.muzeulcotroceni.ro; Tue–Sun 9am–3.30pm), in the Cotroceni district of the city west of the Civic Centre. The area is one of those which largely escaped the communist-era intact. The palace was built in the 1880s for King (then Prince) Ferdinand and his English wife Marie, whose influence is evident everywhere. Located on the site of a former monastery (the foundations and cellars of which remain, and form part of the tour of the palace), the building was designed by a team of French architects, and its design was to become something of a blueprint for Romanian domestic architecture for decades to come. Part of the palace is open to the public, and can be visited on a tour. You will see a number of function rooms as well as Marie's outstanding art collection.

Directly next door to the palace are the Bucharest's **Botanical Gardens** ❹ (Gradina Botanica; www.gradina-botanica.unibuc. ro; gardens: daily 8am–8pm, winter 9am–3.30pm). The gardens, laid out in 1884, are planted with more than 10,000 species, approximately half of which are cultivated in the impressive glasshouses. Look in particular for the exotic flowers, and the bizarre *Symphytum ottomanum*, a plant which disappears without trace only to reappear up to 50m/yds away.

Traditional house in Cotroceni.

EROILOR

There are two notable churches on Strada Sf. Elefterie: the **Old Church of St Elefterus** ㊾ (Biserica Sf. Elefterie Vechi) and the **New Church of St Elefterus** ㊿ (Biserica Sf. Elefterie Nou). The newer church (built 1922) is the very Russian-looking rust and green striped affair, which towers over **Heroes' Square** ㊿ (Piaţa Eroilor). The church has an impressive carved wooden altar and stunning interior frescoes. At 36m (118ft), it is one of the tallest churches in the city. The older, smaller church, which dates from the 1870s, is the more charming, with many of its colourful original frescoes remaining in outstanding condition.

On the northern side of Heroes' Square (across the River Dambovita), and fronted by a small garden and statue of composer George Enescu, is the **Romanian National Opera** (Opera Naţionala Româna). The opera was built from 1950–54 and opened with a performance of Pyotr Tchaikovsky's *Queen of Spades* (the political interests at the time meant that a Russian composer should have the honour).

While the exterior of the building is rather plain, the interior is a different story. The main auditorium is richly decorated and is a superb place to see either opera or ballet (it hosts both). The opera stages first class performances most evenings, and while tickets are very cheap, they can be hard to come by for the more popular operas and ballets.

CISMIGIU

From Heroes' Square a short, rewarding walk west along **Bulevardul Mihai Kogalniceanu** (famed for its Art Nouveau 1920s apartment blocks, many of which are alas in danger of falling during Bucharest's next earthquake: a red disk next to the entrance marks those most at risk) brings you to one of the many entrances of **Cismigiu Gardens** ㊿ (Gradina Cismigiu).

New Church of St Elefterie.

Cismigiu was laid out from 1845–60, and is Bucharest's most centrally located park, busy at all times of day, every day of the year. On summer weekends it can often feel overwhelmingly full. The park's highlights include its artificial lake (on which you can skate in winter – skates can be hired – or row boats in summer), a Roman Garden laid out in the style of Ancient Rome and decorated with busts of Romania's most famous writers, and several large children's play areas. It also has numerous terraces where you can get beer and that classic Romanian snack, *mici*.

BUCHAREST'S OUTSKIRTS

THERME

Since opening in 2015, **Therme București** ❸ (www.therme.ro; Mon–Thurs 10am–11pm, Fri & Sat 9am–midnight, Sun 9am–11pm) has become one of the Romanian capital's leading attractions. The largest thermal bath complex and water park in Central and Eastern Europe, it boasts nine pools and 16 water slides, all served by an underground spring. The inside temperature of the complex is 29°C (84°F) year-round, while the water temperature is a steady 33°C (91°F). There are three separate areas: one with water slides, placing an emphasis on family fun, and two for adults only, geared towards relaxation and wellness. There are innumerable saunas and steam baths, and a variety of massages are also available. During the summer, Europe's largest artificial beach leads into a huge outdoor pool. The complex is around 15km (9 miles) from the centre of Bucharest, and can be reached by bus #442 from Piața Presei, 1km north of the Arc de Triumf. Note that though it's not cheap, you'll have to pay extra if you haven't brought your own towel or flip-flops, both of which are mandatory – and even if you have, they might not be accepted.

SNAGOV

Around 40km (25 miles) from Bucharest, just off the main road to Ploiești, is **Lake Snagov ⬤**, where for centuries some of Romania's

MIHAI EMINESCU

Born Mihail Eminovici, Eminescu was an outrageously handsome romantic poet, journalist and essayist whose tragic early death (he died in 1889 at the age of 38) sealed his place in Romania's artistic pantheon as the country's best loved poet. Though his work is full of melancholy and longing, an overwhelming sense of hope flows from his poetry, not least in his epic work *Luceafărul* (The Evening Star). Romanians study Eminescu throughout their school careers, and most can recite large chunks of his work.

richest people have kept summer houses for centuries. It is immensely popular with the people of Bucharest, who flock here on summer weekends to enjoy the enormous lake, up to 18km (11 miles) long in places and surrounded by the villas of Romania's jet set. You can hire rowing or paddle boats to get a better view of them. The forests that border the lake are popular barbeque venues.

In the middle of the lake is a small island on which stand an impressive **16th-century church** and monastery, and a newer though somewhat shabby wooden church, in which daily services are held for those fit enough to row themselves to the island. The island has been the site of churches since the 11th century, and the present stone church was built in 1521. The body of Vlad Țepes is allegedly buried in the foundations. A small portrait of Vlad marks the spot.

Lake Snagov.

On the bank of the lake opposite the island is **Snagov Palace**, built in 1907 as a summer home for King Carol I. It is notorious as being the location to which Hungarian reformist leader Imre Nagy was taken for intensive questioning after the Hungarian revolution of 1956, before later being tried and executed. Just southeast of Snagov is the impressive **Caldurașani Monastery** (Mănastirea Caldurașani; www.mana-stireacaldarusani.ro), built in 1644–6 during the reign of Matei Basarab. It is famous for its icon-painting school, and it is the monastery's unique collection of icons that most people come to see. Bus #447, which departs from Piața Presei, serves Snagov.

Snagov Palace.

MOGOȘOAIA PALACE

Quite the most impressive sight on the outskirts of Bucharest is the stunning **Mogoșoaia Palace** ⑮ (Palatul Mogoșoaia; www.palatulmogosoaia.ro; Tue–Sun 10am–4pm), found in the *comuna* of Mogoșoaia, about 2km (1.2 miles) beyond the ring road that circles the capital, on the road to Targoviște. The palace was completed in 1702 to the orders of Constantin Brancoveanu, and today houses a museum of superb period furniture and artifacts that once belonged the various owners of the palace. In the grounds is a small Byzantine-style church which predates the palace by 20 years. The golden altar is impressive but not

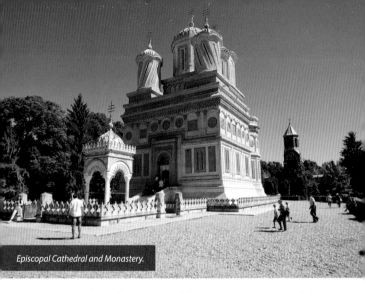

Episcopal Cathedral and Monastery.

original. Also in the grounds of the palace, which are a delight to stroll on summer afternoons and one of few public gardens in Bucharest that welcomes picnickers, you will find the **Bibescu Family Tomb** (the Bibescu family owned the palace from the late 19th century until its expropriation by the state at the end of World War II). You can get to Mogoșoaia on bus #436 from Straulesti metro station.

EXCURSIONS FROM BUCHAREST

All of the excursions we feature are full-day trips from the capital. While Romania's trains are, in general, notoriously slow, upgrades to main lines have at least reduced journey times on the routes from Bucharest to Brașov (through the Prahova Valley) and from Bucharest to Constanța on the Black Sea coast. The journey time to either is now just over two hours.

PITEȘTI AND CURTEA DE ARGEȘ

An hour's drive northwest from the capital along the A1 motorway is the industrial town of Pitești, where Dacia cars are made. There is little to recommend it except a memorial north of the city centre marking the site of Pitești Prison. This – along with Sighet in the very north of Romania – was the most notorious of the communist prisons where countless intellectuals and members of the old ruling class were executed from 1948–54, the darkest years of the Romanian communist regime. Far more pleasant – and what visitors come this way for – is **Curtea de Argeș ㊱**, a small town 38km (24 miles) north of Pitești. It is home to the ruins of the **Princely Court** (Curtea Domneasca; daily 10am–5pm) built by Basarab I in the 14th century. There is little left of the court building, but its superbly preserved church (Biserica Domneasca) is in fine fettle and open to the public at all hours. Basarab I, an early ruler of Wallachia, is buried near the church's altar. Romania's last king, Mihai, was also buried here on his death in 2017. A short distance north of the city is the even more impressive **Episcopal Cathedral and Monastery** (Catedrala Episcopala Curtea de Arges). A classic piece of Byzantine architecture, the cathedral was built between 1514 and 1526 using materials brought almost entirely from Constantinople, on the orders of Neagoe Basarab, the son of Basarab I. Curtea de Argeș is the southern starting point of the **Transfagarașan Highway**.

SINAIA

Set at a cooling 800m (2,625ft), and originally the mountain retreat of kings and hermit monks, **Sinaia ㊲** (which takes its name from the 17th-century Sinaia Monastery, in turn named after Mount Sinai) can today be reached in 90 minutes on the train from Bucharest. The skiing here, high up at 2,000m (6,562ft), accessed by a two-stage cable car and a gondola, is the best and most challenging in the country, and there is often enough snow for skiing as late as May. When the snow is particularly good you can ski all the way down to Sinaia itself, a good 12km (7 miles). During the summer there are fantastic walks in the Bucegi Mountains, which are crisscrossed with hundreds of well-marked routes. The less energetic can access the mountains by the cable car or gondola, which operates year-round.

Sinaia is also home to two exquisite sights: Sinaia Monastery and Peleş Castle. A short walk through Sinaia's main park, at the end of its main street, Bulevardul Carol I, will bring you to the stunning **Sinaia Monastery** (Mănastirea Sinaia; Wed–Sun 10am–6pm), founded by Prince Mihai Cantacuzino in 1682 after a pilgrimage to Mount Sinai and the Holy Land. There are two churches: Biserica Veche (Old Church) dating from 1695, and Biserica Mare (Great Church), built in 1846.

Peleş Castle (Castelul Peleş; tours Wed–Sun 9am–3pm), designed in an extraordinary Germanic, neo-Renaissance style, is

THE TRANSFAGARAŞAN HIGHWAY

The Transfagaraşan Highway was made famous globally by an appearance in an episode of *Top Gear*, and has since become a rite of passage for drivers and motorcyclists from across Europe. The highway begins to the north of Curtea de Argeş, and climbs its way over and across the Carpathian Mountains, reaching a height of 2,042m (6,699ft). The road is fully open for only a few months each year due to snowfall, and snow can still block roads in June. While the road can make for a perfect day trip from Bucharest, you will need your own transport; avoid the weekends, when half of Romania turns up, and one of the most spectacular drives in the world resembles a giant zig-zag car park.

Piaţa Sfatului, Braşov.

situated in the cool conifer forests above the town. It was built to order from 1874 to 1883 for Romania's first modern king, Carol I, who used it as his summer residence. Tours of the castle are available in any number of languages. The smaller **Pelişor** complex in the grounds (Wed–Sun 9am–3pm; admission included in ticket for main castle) was the preferred mountain retreat of Queen Marie, English wife of Carol's successor, Ferdinand.

BRAŞOV

Braşov ⑤, set at an altitude of 600m, is a town in two parts: Old Braşov, comprising the old walled Saxon city; and new Braşov: all bleak apartment blocks and polluting factories. Both parts of the city stand in the shadow of the enormous Tâmpa Mountain. Luckily, once you have arrived you need never leave the older parts of town.

Most visitors begin their time in Braşov with a walk along **Bulevardul Republicii**, a cobbled, pedestrianised street that leads to **Piaţa Sfatului**, the heart of the Old Town. Before you do, however, duck into the excellent **Ethnography Museum** (Muzeul de Etnografie; Wed–Sat 10am–5pm) on Bulevardul Eroilor, and the small but charming **Art Museum** (Muzeul de Arta; Tue–Sun 10am–6pm) next to it. The Art Museum has a particularly good selection of paintings by 19th-century impressionist Nicolae Grigorescu. A little further along is the remarkable Art Deco **Aro Palace Hotel**.

During the summer Bulevardul Republicii is packed with street cafés and terraces leading all the way up to, and around, Piaţa Sfatului. This large square, which the Saxons called Marktplatz, is dominated by the old Casa Sfatului (Council Hall) that stands in the middle. It was built in 1420, though the tower, once used as a lookout post for approaching Ottomans, is slightly older. A few steps from Piaţa Sfatului is the single most impressive sight in Braşov, the

The Constanta Casino.

Black Church (Biserica Neagra; Mon–Sat 10am–4pm). First called the Marienkirche and built from 1385 to 1477, it was blackened during a fire in 1689 that destroyed much of the city. It has been known as the Black Church ever since. The church boasts the largest organ in the country, and organ concerts are held most summer Sundays.

CONSTANȚA

An important Black Sea port throughout its 2,000-year history, modern **Constanța** 59 is one of Europe's largest working ports. There are oil refineries in the region too, making the city one of the wealthiest in Romania. Despite all the heavy industry, Constanța is nevertheless a popular holiday resort in its own right, with a splendid beach and much to see – mainly its ancient walls, relics and the museums that house them. Start off in the heart of old Tomis at Piața Ovidiu, named for the Latin poet Ovidiu, who was exiled to the neighbouring resort of Mamaia (a statue of the poet stands in the middle of the square), and its spacious, informative **Museum of National History and Archeology** (Muzeul de Istorie Nationala si Arheologie; Tue–Sun 10am–4pm). Slightly behind the museum are the remnants of a stunning Roman mosaic (Tue–Sun 10am–6pm) discovered in 1959. A short walk south of the square is the most impressive of Constanța's two working mosques, the **Mahmudiye Mosque**, whose 55m (180ft) minaret is open to visitors (Sat–Thu 10am–5pm). The vast and somewhat subdued **Romanian Orthodox Cathedral** (Catedrala Ortodoxa) is only slightly further on, and just beyond lies the seafront. It's enjoyable enough just walking along here, as the promenade is wide and inviting, and during the evening there is quite a procession of courting couples and families. The much photographed but sadly run-down casino –built in 1909, when Constanța was one of Europe's leading seaside resorts – is easy to spot; renovation was ongoing at the time of writing.

Bike tour of the city.

THINGS TO DO

SPORTS

FOOTBALL

Football is the national sport, and Bucharest is home to three of the country's most popular teams: Steaua (who won the European Cup in 1986, and are now officially known as FCSB), Dinamo and Rapid. Derbies attract big crowds to the national stadium, the Arena Naționala, where Steaua play their home matches. Tickets are cheap and be purchased online on a few of the main international ticketing sites, or at the stadium on the day of games. Check the SuperLiga site (www.lpf.ro) for fixture information.

SWIMMING AND LAKE ACTIVITIES

Bucharest is home to Central and Eastern Europe's largest thermal bath complex, **Therme București** (see page 66), which is open until late every day. There is a small but quite spectacular pool on the top floor of the **Grand** hotel (see page 122), while the **Radisson Blu** (see page 124) opens its large outdoor pool to the public during the summer. In Herăstrău Park, **Zexe** (www.zexeherastrau.ro) rents out SUPs, kayaks and sailboats.

CYCLING AND SCOOTERS

Cycling has long been viewed by locals as a means of transport for people who can't afford cars, rather than a recreational activity. There are a few marked cycling routes in the city, however, and all of the city's large parks now have paths for cyclists, the best and longest being at Herăstrău, where the cycling path circumnavigates the lake. You can hire bikes at the main entrance to the park at Piața

Charles de Gaulle, but you will need to bring ID. Bucharest has also joined the ranks of cities in which app-based scooters are left all over the pavements; Bolt (www.bolt.eu) is probably your best bet.

GOLF

There is an 18-hole, championship-grade golf course at **Bucharest Golf Club** (www.bucharest.golf), on the fringes of Snagov Lake (see page 67). In the city proper, you could give the under-used Diplomatic course in Herăstrău Park a go; otherwise, mini-golf is the only choice.

SKIING

Bucharest is flat, as is the surrounding area, but there is good, challenging skiing less than two hours away at **Sinaia** in the Prahova Valley. There are around 25km (15 miles) of slopes, and snow can usually be guaranteed from the beginning of December until the middle of April, although the highest slopes at Sinaia – which are above 2,000m (6,560ft) – often stay open as late as mid-May. If you get an early train from Gara de Nord, you can be on the slopes at Sinaia by 9am. There are plenty of places to rent kit, and prices for equipment and the ski lifts are relatively low by Western European standards.

HIKING

Hiking is just about the most popular physical activity in Romania. When the snow has melted, Sinaia and neighbouring Buşteni become popular hiking centres, and there are hundreds of routes of varying difficulty which criss-cross the mountains, all of which are well-marked and well-maintained. Small mountain huts provide cheap refreshments, including basic cooked meals. Some offer beds for the night. The weather in the mountains can be changeable even on what appear to be sunny summer days. Bring rain jackets

Skiing in Sinaia.

and do not venture into the mountains if the forecast is poor: it can occasionally snow on the highest peaks, even during summer.

SHOPPING

Large shopping malls dot the city, and offer a retail experience little different to that found anywhere else in Europe. All contain instantly recognisable major high street clothing, cosmetics and sports brands you would expect to find in any mall across Europe, as well as local chains, cinemas and entertainment complexes, and food courts.

The **AFI Cotroceni** (Bulevardul General Vasile Milea 4; www.afi-cotroceni.ro) in the west of the city, which includes a small indoor rollercoaster, a large ice skating rink and the **Museum of Senses** (www.museumofsenses.ro), a hands-on cornucopia of experiments and sensations kids will love, is the city's largest mall. It is closely followed by **Baneasa Shopping City** (Șoseaua București-Ploiești 42D; www.baneasa.ro), to the north of the city centre, which boasts the country's largest cinema complex. Other malls of note include **Park Lake** (Strada Liviu Rebreanu 4; www.parklake.ro), set in a beautiful location in the east of the city on the edge of one of Bucharest's largest parks, and the **Promenada Mall** (www.promenada.ro) close to Aurel Vlaicu metro station, which has a rooftop recreation area that during the summer shows films and hosts live music.

Slightly different is **Unirea Shopping Centre** (www.unireashop.ro) on Piața Unirii in the city centre. Originally built in the 1970s as a showpiece of communist consumerism, it was for decades packed with goods few people wanted to buy and bereft of anything they actually did. It has since been extended, and is today a slightly haphazard mix of big name retail stores and smaller boutiques.

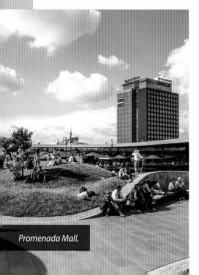

Promenada Mall.

High street shopping has had to take something of a back seat to the malls, but a couple of worthwhile shopping areas remain, especially if you are looking for high-end goods. On a short strip of **Calea Victoriei** around the Athénée Palace Hilton and Radisson Blu hotels you will find couture labels such as Burberry, Gucci and Max Mara, as well as the showrooms of Romanian designers, while a number of quirky antiques shops are centered on **Hanul cu Tei** in the Old Town area.

Bucharest's best market is **Bucur Obor** (take the metro to Obor), a huge market selling everything from fruit and vegetables to fishing tackle and spare parts for cars. There is a **flea market** every Sunday morning in Vitan, south of the city centre. There is also a small **antiques market** every Saturday and Sunday at the main entrance to Carol Park.

> ### Flower etiquette
>
> If you feel the urge to give somebody flowers while in Bucharest make sure you hand over an odd number of blooms. Even numbered bunches of flowers are usually given only at funerals in Romania, and are considered bad luck.

WHAT TO BUY

Traditional Romanian handicrafts worth seeking out include embroidery, pottery, wood carvings and iconography. Romanian souvenir shops are ubiquitous, especially in the Old Town, although the souvenirs in many of them can be of patchy quality, often little more than Chinese-made trinkets with Dracula motifs emblazoned on them.

Beautiful **Orthodox icons**, especially those hand-painted on glass or wood, can be found at the large shops inside the Peasant Museum (see page 56) and at the Village Museum (see page 62). These two stores source all of their goods from renowned craftspeople and artisans across Romania, and while prices are far from cheap, it is guaranteed that quality will be high. The two shops also sell **hand-painted Easter eggs** (which make fabulous souvenirs if you can get them home intact) and intricately embroidered **Romanian blouses**, known as *ie*. You will find much cheaper blouses in stores across the city but they are likely to be cheap reproductions.

Traditional Romanian pottery.

There's fine **Romanian porcelain** for sale at **Art Time Atelier** (Strada Popa Nan 10; www.arttime.ro), where you can even get hands-on and create your own designs.

Bucharest's most visited shop, however, is **Cartureşti Carusel** (Strada Lipscani 55; www.carturesti.ro) in the Old Town, which, besides being a fine book and gift store (with a good selection of books about Bucharest and Romania in English), attracts hordes of tourists eager to see (and photograph) its jaw-dropping interior. There is a good café on the top floor (see page 103).

FOOD AND DRINK

The Belgian-owned Mega Image chain of supermarkets dominates Bucharest, with stores on almost every major street. Besides everyday groceries, they also stock a good range of Romanian wine, beer, cheese and salami. Vinexpert (Bulevardul Octavian Goga 24; www.vinexpert.ro), a short walk east from Piaţa Unirii, has an outstanding selection of fine Romanian and Moldovan wines and spirits. Try to avoid buying wine at the overpriced duty-free shops at Henri Coanda International Airport.

ENTERTAINMENT

OPERA, CLASSICAL MUSIC AND BALLET

Opera has a long history in Romania, and it is enjoyed by a surprisingly wide variety of people, of all ages. The country has provided the world of opera with a large number of prima donnas, from Haricleea Darclee in the late 19th century to the incomparable Angela Gheorghiu, whose magnetic voice has seen her top the bill at Covent Garden hundreds of times since her debut in 1992. Alina Cojocaru, principal dancer with the English National Ballet, was born in Bucharest, and recently returned for a short season at the Romanian National Opera. Romania's national composer is George Enescu, better known outside of Romania as Georges Enesco. His best-known work is the *Romanian Rhapsody*, written while he was living in Paris in 1901. He was just 20 at the time. Bucharest's philharmonic orchestra, created as long ago as 1777, is

BUCHAREST MONOPOLY

Featuring Rahova as the cheapest property and Primaverii as the most expensive, the Bucharest version of Monopoly makes a brilliant gift. It's full of quirks, just like the original, not least the fact that three of the four train stations no longer serve rail passengers, and you can still win money by coming second in a beauty contest. All book and toy stores stock the game, including Diverta, a book and stationery chain found in all of the city's malls.

based at the Ateneul Român and was renamed the George Enescu Philharmonic Orchestra following his death in 1955.

Two venues dominate the music scene in Bucharest: the **Romanian National Opera** (Bulevardul Mihail Kogălniceanu 70–72; www.operanb.ro), home of opera and ballet, and the **Ateneul Român** (Strada Benjamin Franklin 1–3; www.fge.org.ro), Romania's leading classical music venue and home of its best orchestra. Performances at both venues are always outstanding but while tickets are very cheap by western European standards, they can often be hard to come by. Make sure you reserve well in advance (both venues offer online ticket purchase on their websites). The **Sala Radio** (Strada General H.M. Berthelot 60–64; www.orchestreradio.ro) close to Cismigiu Park also hosts classical music, and has become well-known for its smaller scale concerts,

George Enescu Festival.

particularly chamber music recitals. Every two years, Bucharest hosts the **George Enescu Festival** (www.festivalenescu.ro) a month-long extravaganza of classical music which attracts the best orchestras, soloists and conductors from across the world. Tickets need to be purchased months in advance.

THEATRE

The **National Theatre** (Bulevardul Nicolae Bălcescu 2; www.tnb.ro) hosts classical theatre, almost exclusively in Romanian, although local productions of popular Broadway musicals occasionally enjoy short runs. There is a fair amount of contemporary dance, as well as comedy, at the **Odeon Theatre** (Calea Victoriei 40–42; www.teatrul-odeon.ro), while the **Small Theatre** (Strada Constantin Mille 16; www.teatrulmic.ro) is a great place to watch more intimate productions.

CINEMA

The good news is that foreign-language films are not dubbed – they are usually screened in the original language, with subtitles. The main exceptions are children's animated films, but even these usually have the option of a subtitled version. If the word *dublat* appears next to a film's name it will be dubbed, *subtitrat* means subtitled. All of the city's shopping malls have large multiplex cinemas.

ROCK AND POP

Bucharest is now a regular stop for performers on European tours. The biggest concerts are held in Piața Constituției directly in front of the Palace of Parliament, or at the national stadium, the Arena Naționala. Smaller gigs are hosted at Sala Palatului (Strada Ion Câmpineanu 28; www.salapalatului.ro) or the Arenele Romane inside Carol Park south of Piața Unirii. Tickets can be purchased

Hanul lui Manuc.

online at www.bilete.ro or www.iabilet.ro, or from branches of Diverta, which can be found in all of the big shopping malls.

Local rock and pop acts perform regularly at Bucharest's Hard Rock Cafe on the edge of Herăstrău Park (www.hardrockcafe.com), or at Berarie H (www.berariah.ro) opposite. However, during the summer and on national holidays there are often free live concerts featuring local acts in Bucharest (and indeed around Romania), paid for by local councils and held in public squares.

TRADITIONAL MUSIC

Listening to a Gypsy band, a *taraf*, should be high on the list of any visitor to Bucharest. They play traditional Romanian music mixed with faster Gypsy rhythms to create what is known as *muzică lăutărească* (which roughly translates as fiddler's music). **True Club** (Strada Covaci 19; www.trueclub.ro) in the Old Town regularly hosts these bands, including the popular Taraf de Caliu. A number of Bucharest's traditional Romanian restaurants, such as **Caru cu Bere** (see page 103) and **Hanul lui Manuc** (see page 104) have resident bands performing most evenings. At Hanul lui Manuc these concerts take place in the courtyard during the summer.

CLUBS AND BARS

Bucharest's nightlife scene is one of the very best in Europe. A number of enormous venues accommodating thousands of clubbers from across Europe and the Middle East attract big name DJs from around the world. The best of these are **BOA** (Șoseaua Kiseleff 32; www.boa-beatofangels.com) and **Oxya** (Strada Caroteni 13; www.oxya.ro). These clubs are usually open only on Friday and Saturday nights, from around midnight until late the next morning. Note that the Bucharest clubbing scene shuts down during July and August, when things decamp to Mamaia, near Constanța on the Black Sea coast.

Lower-key clubs include **Control** (Strada Constantin Mille 4; www.control-club.ro), which puts on alternative music nights and hosts live bands a couple of times a week, and **Beat Bar Umanist** (Strada Vasile Lascar 29), one of very few places in Bucharest where you can regularly expect to find live jazz. **Mojo** (Strada Gabroveni 14; www.mojomusic.ro) puts on live local bands every weekend, as well as occasional English-language stand-up comedy and quiz nights. **Zăganu** (Calea Victoriei 91–93; www.bere-zaganu.ro) has a wide selection of their own craft beers, but for a wider choice try **Ground Zero** (Toma Caragiu 3; www.groundzerobeer.ro) in the Old Town. **Cork's Cozy Bar**, also in the Old Town (Strada Bacani 1; www.corks.ro), is a gorgeous little wine bar with an amazing selection, almost all available by the glass. Lastly, you could try **Clique** (Bulevardul Unirii 31; www.theclique.ro), the only resto-bar on the riverfront that hasn't automatically given their prime seating to smokers; or **Piana Vyshnia** (Strada Covaci 3; www.pianavyshnia.com), a remote branch of a Ukrainian cherry-brandy bar chain (the cherries, soaked in alcohol, will give you a momentary buzz).

CHILDREN'S BUCHAREST

There are loads of things for children to do in Bucharest. As good a place as any to start is the **Village Museum** (see page 62), its many houses, windmills and wooden churches – all of which can be explored – will fascinate young minds. For children who want a more hands-on experience there are often activities on summer weekends, including an introduction to local crafts such as pottery and egg painting. The excellent confectionery stall at the entrance, selling home-made sweets, cakes and suchlike, will also be a hit.

Surrounding the museum is **Herăstrău Park**, which has a number of attractions for children, including boat rides on the lake during the summer, or pedal boats for the energetic. Bikes are available for hire, and there are large playgrounds suitable for younger children.

Playing football in Herăstrău Park.

To really give the kids a treat though, jump on the metro and head for **Oraşelul Copiilor** (Children's City; take the metro to Constantin Brancoveanu station). The entire park is given over to children's activities: there are playgrounds, boating lakes, a miniature railway,

Bucharest City Tour bus.

bouncy castles and a large funfair, complete with big wheel and rides of varying scariness for all ages.

The **National Technical Museum** (Strada Candiano Popescu 2; www.mnt-leonida.ro) is somewhat outdated but packed with crazy inventions (including an early attempt to create a jetpack), steam engines, model trains and electronics that will keep kids occupied for hours. There is also a science theme at the **Museum of Senses** in the AFI Palace Cotroceni shopping mall.

The **Romanian National Opera** (see page 65) puts on children's matinees most weekend mornings at 11am, and there are puppet shows on Saturday mornings at the **Peasant Museum** (see page 56).

Outside of the city, **Therme București** (see page 66) has water slides, swimming pools and – during the summer – a large outdoor beach, while at **Edenland** (www.edenland.ro), located in a forest north of Bucharest, there is a huge range of adventure trails as well as paintball, archery and other outdoor activities.

CALENDAR OF EVENTS

January New Year's Day is celebrated by groups of young men who wander through the city in sheepskins – and sometimes even bearskins – singing, dancing and banging drums, collecting money from onlookers. St John's Day (Sf. Ioan) on 7 January sees churches packed with the faithful waiting to receive blessed water from priests.

March The Jazz in Church festival brings world-class performers to the Lutheran Church in central Bucharest.

April Orthodox Easter – which falls according to the Gregorian calendar – is the most important religious event of the year. The Spotlight Bucharest Light Festival sees light-based installations take over Calea Victoriei.

May The Bucharest International Jazz Festival is held at various venues across the city, with street performances in the Old Town. East European Comic Con is the region's largest celebration of popular culture. Revino Wine Show, Romania's premier wine event, takes place over a weekend.

June Romanian Design Week showcases Romania's creative industries at venues across the city. Street Delivery celebrates local artists and NGOs over three days at Strada Artur Verona.

July Summer Well is a huge music festival held over four days at Buftea, 20km (12 miles) northwest of Bucharest.

August The Bucharest Craft Beer Festival brings together craft brewers from across Romania and neighbouring countries. The Bucharest Air Show offers aerial thrills at the otherwise little-used Baneasa Airport.

September The George Enescu Classical Music Festival takes place at venues throughout the city every odd-numbered year.

October Art Safari is a huge urban art festival of contemporary art. The main exhibition site is Piața Revoluției. Revino Gourmet Show, at the end of the month, is chance to sample Romania's finest cheeses, cured meats and wines.

November–December Large Christmas markets set up shop in mid-November in Piața Universității and Piața Constituției. Romania's National Day, 1 December, is celebrated with a huge military display around the Arc de Triumf.

FOOD AND DRINK

The quality of food served in Bucharest's restaurants continues to improve: young, innovative chefs are rethinking the country's somewhat unadventurous cuisine and taking it to new levels of invention, creating a New Romanian Wave based on local, seasonal ingredients. While it can be argued that the best Romanian food is usually eaten in family homes, where you can be sure that only the freshest and best ingredients have been used, this is changing, especially in the capital.

Besides the array of Romanian restaurants, lovers of Italian food are in for a treat as the city boasts a considerable number of great Italian eateries, many of which were opened by Romanian emigrants to Italy who have returned home.

WHERE TO EAT

It took many years after the 1989 revolution before Romania really began to get serious about eating out. As late as 2010 there were few places where you could eat well anywhere in the country, but there has been a veritable explosion of great restaurants since then. Bucharest unquestionably has the best selection of places to eat in the country, with prices, even at the high-end restaurants, that remain low by western European standards. The cosmopolitan city now offers restaurants of every cuisine imaginable, from Japanese to Indian to the latest in cutting-edge French-Asian Fusion. Portions can often be huge.

Children, not long ago entirely absent from restaurants, are now more than welcome and most places offer a special children's menu. During the summer, locals love nothing more than eating al fresco, and restaurants which do not provide a terrace, courtyard or garden struggle to attract clients.

Traditional Romanian breakfast.

For an authentic taste of Romania, you should try and get yourself invited to a Romanian home; the food and drink will not stop coming until you insist that you can eat or drink no more. If you do find yourself invited to a home, be sure to bring flowers (see page 81).

WHEN TO EAT

Romanians tend to eat light breakfasts very early – often just coffee with bread, cheese and ham or salami – followed by an early lunch of considerable proportions. That being said, most hotels, even some cheaper establishments, offer lavish breakfast buffets. Until recently, lunch was the primary meal of the day in Bucharest, while evening meals were often an afterthought and eaten much later in the evening. Nowadays things have changed to the extent that many restaurants, including some of the best, try to tempt customers in with cheap lunch deals, which often feature three or four courses – fantastic for visitors, who are advised to make lunch their main meal.

Restaurants in Romania usually open for lunch around 11am and stay open until late at night. They rarely close during the afternoon.

POPULAR DISHES

Romanians claim a wide variety of dishes as their own, only for the visitor to find the same thing all over the Balkans. Many of the most famous national dishes will be familiar to the traveller who has visited Turkey, Bulgaria or the former Yugoslavia, only under slightly different names.

Starters (antreuri)

Romania is famous for its *ciorbe* – sour soups made with *borş* (a sour, honey-coloured liquid made of wheat and cornflour). In theory, anything can go into a ciorba, though the most popular are *ciorba de legume* (made with vegetables), *ciorba de vacuta* (made with beef), *ciorba de burta* (made with tripe), *ciorba de perişoare* (made with pork meatballs) or *borş de miel* (made with lamb, popular at Easter). While you will often see *ciorba de pui* (ciorba made with chicken), chicken is more popular in clear soups, served with tough but tasty little dumplings (*galuşte*), carrots and parsnips.

Meat and vegetable soup.

Other popular starters include platters of cold cuts and sausage (*gustări rece*) served with cheese, spring onions and tomatoes, and big Greek-style salads (*salate*). Fried chicken livers (*ficaţei de pui*) with onion and mushrooms and topped with heaps of parsley can be eaten either as a starter or main course.

Meat Dishes

The Romanian staple is pork (*porc*), and it is simply superb, both in taste and texture. You will find it served in a variety of ways, though to sample its succulent flavour a steak, grilled on an open fire, is arguably the best. It is also delicious when roasted on the bone, and served with a bean stew (*iahnie de fasole*) – the dish is called *ciolan de porc cu fasole*. Chicken (*pui*) in Romania is equally common, though nowhere near as good in quality. Beef (*vita*) is

Kebabs and mici.

found widely, but its quality is similarly unreliable, often poor, and typically imported when served in the top restaurants. Lamb (*miel*) is difficult to find, except at Easter when it forms the base of the Easter meal. Romanian game, notably duck (*rața*) and goose (*gâsca*), is found on good restaurant menus and is usually of a high standard.

Kadayif, a popular Turkish dessert.

The most famous dish of Romania is undeniably *sarmale* (cabbage or vine leaves stuffed with pork mince and rice), served with *mamaliga*, a Romanian version of polenta made of cornmeal (its characteristic stodginess has long been compared to the Romanian temperament). *Sarmale cu mamaliga* is best found on the menus of traditional Romanian restaurants, though you could also try cheaper soup-shops or canteens, or even put the ingredients together at a supermarket.

You should also not leave Romania without tasting *mici*: small, reasonably spicy sausage-shaped meatballs – usually a mixture of pork and mutton but sometimes pork and beef – which are grilled on an open fire and served with bread and mustard. Though found all over Romania, those made in Bucharest and in the south of the country are beyond compare. The aroma of them cooking in markets and on terraces is impossible to resist.

Transylvanian specialities, popular in Bucharest, include *tocanița* (stew), either chicken, pork or beef, cooked slowly for hours in a hotpot with generous amounts of paprika, betraying the enduring Hungarian influence in the region.

Fish

With a prominent coastline and numerous inland lakes and waterways, you would expect Romania to be a fish-loving country. The reality is quite different: Carp (*crap*) is eaten occasionally, usually grilled and simmered in a sour sauce called *saramură*, as is trout (*pastrav*) and pikeperch (*salau*).

On the other hand, there are some very good seafood restaurants in Bucharest, but they serve imported fish at relatively high prices. Nonetheless, Romania has a wonderful tradition of producing and eating fish roe, known as *icre*, which is usually mixed with garlic, onion and mayonnaise and served as a delicious spread.

Romanian winery.

Bread

Romanian bread (*pâine*) can be poor as it is often made with cheap flour, though don't forego *covrigi* – plain bread bagels sold on street corners everywhere, covered in salt and delicious when piping hot. They're one of the items on offer at branches of Luca, a local bakery chain that's almost tantamount to a religion – there are queues outside most branches clean through the day.

Dessert

When it comes to dessert, Romanians have a very sweet tooth – partly the Turkish influence. Baklava is common in Bucharest, while *cozonac*, sweet bread with chocolate or raisins is popular all over the country, all year round, especially at Easter and Christmas. Romanians also love *gogoşi* – plain donuts, served hot and crispy with *smântana* (sour cream). *Papanaşi* are smaller donuts, usually filled with jam. You will also come across *plăcinte* – fried pies stuffed with jam or cheese and topped with sour cream – which are best eaten piping-hot and bought from small bakeries dotted around the city.

Vegetarians and Vegans

Vegetarians and vegans are surprisingly well catered for, as many Romanians still observe lent, both in the month before Easter and before Christmas, as well as on all Wednesdays and Fridays. At these times, restaurants offer food that fits the strict rules of the Romanian Orthodox Church – no meat, fish or dairy products. Look out for the sign, 'Avem produse de post' (lent menu available).

Romanian cuisine has a number of vegan specialities, including borş de loboda (a kind of sour soup), rice-stuffed peppers, *iahnie de fasole* (bean stew) and *dovlecei* (fried courgettes). Another popular vegan delicacy is *vinete*, a salad made from grilled aubergines and served spread on bread. Aubergines are also popular grilled and served pickled in oil and vinegar. Another vegan spread is *zacuska*, (a delicious chutney made of tomatoes, peppers, mushrooms and onions), which is usually eaten at breakfast. There are also now vegan versions of the national dish, *sarmale* (see page 95).

Fruit and vegetables are an integral part of Romanian cuisine. Strictly seasonal, they have real flavour and taste superb, with much of the produce intrinsically organic. Tomatoes especially have a taste that long ago disappeared from the supermarkets of Western Europe. Sweetcorn (*porumb*) is popular in season (July, August and early September), and you will find street vendors selling boiled cobs. Melons, both water (*pepene*) and honeydew (*pepene galben*), are fabulous, and appear at the end of July. Prices are high at the beginning of the season, but by the end of September they are all but given away. From May to July, Romania's new potatoes (*cartofi noi*) are stunning, and fresh Romanian cabbage (*varza*) will change your entire perception of that erstwhile tired, old vegetable.

WHAT TO DRINK

Now for the really good news: Romania is a wine- and beer-producing country, and prices are low. Almost 2 percent of the total agricultural land in Romania is given over to vineyards, making the country one of the top 10 wine producers globally. Local spirits are often lethal, and not for the faint of heart.

Wine (Vin)

Romania has been producing wine since Dacian times, and has eight major wine-producing regions. Moldavia is the largest and best known. As a general rule, the best whites are made in the north, while the highest quality reds of Romania are made in the south. There are many exceptions, however. While Romania grows international varieties of grape, from Sauvignon Blanc to Merlot,

Csíki Sör beers.

the country also boasts a number of excellent native grapes. The best local varieties are probably the noble, blackcurrant-tinged *Feteasca Neagra* (red), *Feteasca Alba* (white), *Feteasca Regala* (white) and the aromatic, honey-like *Tamaioasa Romaneasca* (white).

Labels from reliable wineries to look out for include Halewood, Domeniile Tohani, Murfatlar, Davino, Stirbey, Corcova and Domeniul Coroanei. You might also want to try *Busuioacă de Bohotin* which, while too sweet for many tastes, is a unique Romanian wine and one of the few decent roses made in the country. It is very popular during the summer. Another unique Romanian wine is *Lacrima lui Ovidiu* – a bold, strong, yet sweet wine from Murfatlar, made from grapes harvested deliberately late. Note that prices of Romanian wine almost always reflect quality, so you are advised to spend as much as possible when making a selection.

All good Bucharest restaurants now stock an excellent range of imported wines, especially from France and Italy.

Beer (Bere)

There has never been a better time to be a beer drinker in Romania, as the country has taken to the craft beer revolution in a major way and now produces some outstanding brews.

Of the better-known beers, Ursus is the most popular and as close as the country has to a national beer. Timisoreana is also good, especially the unfiltered variety. Other popular beers, which you will immediately spot as being ubiquitous, include Ciuc, Tuborg, Bergenbier and the slightly less common Silva, which produces a good pale ale.

Craft beers – the first of which appeared only in 2013 – include Zaganu, produced in small quantities at their brewery in the Carpathian Mountains near Cheia, not far from Brașov. Its IPA, a Belgian-style red ale, is superb. Sikaru is the other brand of craft

Plum pălincă.

beer to watch out for – and its summer ale is perhaps the best beer brewed in Romania. In the Old Town, Strada Gabroveni is known as Strada Di Bere (Beer Street), as three great craft beer bars stand in a row. Imported beers are available in most bars.

No cheese please!

For some unexplained reason, Romanians usually serve their fries covered with grated cheese. When ordering you can avoid this by stating, '*fara branza pe cartofi prajiți, vă rog*'.

Cider (Cidru)

Clark's, brewed by a Scotsman using only local apples, was Romania's first real cider. Very popular in Bucharest, and found in many bars and pubs, it is available in dry, medium dry or medium sweet varieties.

Spirits (Tarie)

The most famous local spirits are *țuică* and its slightly more refined counterpart, *pălincă*. Both are made with plums and are incredibly strong. The taste, once you are used to it, can be surprisingly good. Though they are produced and sold commercially, the home-made variety is far better. Most Romanians have a family member in the countryside who can procure the genuine article.

Coffee (Cafea)

Coffee was scarce during the Communist period and considered a luxury, which might explain why it has since become almost the national drink. Bucharest boasts more speciality coffee shops per head than any other city in Europe. On the other end of the scale, you'll find chains (such as the ubiquitous 5 To Go) selling decent-enough espresso drinks at rock-bottom prices; some are just holes in the wall, while others have proper seats and tables.

TO HELP YOU ORDER...

Could we have a table? Ne puteți oferi o masă?
I'd like a/an/some... Aș dori o/niște…
The bill, please. Nota, vă rog.

apple măr	**orange** portocală
beans fasole	**peach** piersică
bread pâine	**peas** mazăre
butter unt	**pepper** piper
cake prăjitură	**pineapple** ananas
carrots morcovi	**pork** porc
cheese brânză	**potatoes** cartofi
cherries cireși	**prawns** creveți
chicken pui	**rice** orez
coffee cafea	**salad** salată
dessert desert	**sandwich** sandviș
egg ou	**sauce** sos
figs smochine	**sea bass** biban de mare
fish pește	**shellfish** crustacea
fillet filet	**soup** supă
fruit fructe	**squid** calamar
garlic usturoi	**strawberries** căpșune
grapes struguri	**sugar** zahăr
ham șuncă	**shellfish** crustacea
ice cream înghețată	**stewed/braised** fript înăbușit
lamb miel	
mackerel macrou	**steak (beef)** friptură (vită)
meat carne	**stew** tocană
milk lapte	**tuna** ton
mushrooms ciuperci	**turkey** curcan
mussels midii	**tea** ceai
olives măsline	**trout** păstrăv
onion ceapă	**wine** vin

WHERE TO EAT

We have used the following symbols to give an idea of the price for a three-course meal for two, without wine:

€€€	over €40
€€	€20–40
€	under €20

PIAȚA UNIVERSITĂȚII AND THE OLD TOWN

Animaletto House €€ *Strada Dianei 4, tel: 074-817 7115*. This charming Italian restaurant is a short walk from Piața Universității, and boasts one of the most gorgeous courtyards in the city – perfect for long evenings, enjoying lobster soup or truffle pasta, and sipping some fine wine.

Bazaar €€ *Strada Covaci 10, tel: 072-199 9999,* www.thebazaar.ro. A wide variety of food from across the globe, including a decent attempt at fish and chips, as well as traditional Romanian classics and great burgers. Attractively designed, with a huge terrace on one of the busiest streets in the Old Town.

Caru cu Bere €€ *Strada Stavropoleos 5, tel: 021-313 75 60,* www.carucubere. ro. A symbol of Bucharest that should be on every visitor to-do list, 'Beer Cart', offers good local food and a wide selection of Romanian and international beer – including their own brew in an Art Nouveau-style building. Cheap, filling lunch deals on weekdays.

Carusel Café € *Strada Lipscani 55, tel: 072-882 8922,* https://carturesti.ro. On the top floor of the elegant Carturesti Carusel bookshop, offering a wide range of quirky drinks, delicious food, coffee and hot chocolate. A great place to while away an hour in the Old Town.

Gyros Thessalonikis € *Strada Gabroveni 2, tel: 073-083 0336*. Serving the best kebabs in the Old Town, at prices no higher than so-so spots in the suburbs, this place offers superb lamb, pork or chicken gyros and souvlaki, plus Greek beers. They've a pleasant terrace, and occasional live Greek music.

Hanu' lui Manuc €€ *Strada Franceză 62–64, tel: 073-018 8653,* www.hanu manucrestaurant.ro. The standard Romanian fare here is good, if not extraordinary, and few places in Bucharest provide an experience as authentically Wallachian, particularly in the summer when you can sit in the large courtyard. They offer cheap lunch deals on weekdays; you may need a reservation at weekends.

Lacrimi si Sfinti €€ *Strada Șepcari 16, tel: 072-555 8286,* www.lacrimisisfinti. com. Owned by Mircea Dinescu, one of Romania's best-loved poets and raconteurs, you'll find a wide range of local produce on the menu here, including game (the duck is always sensational) from Dinescu's own estate, as well as the many fine wines from his own vineyards. Talented musicians serenade diners most evenings.

Lente €€ *Strada Arcului 8, tel: 021-210 9696,* www.lente.ro. Tucked away at the end of an alleyway, this sublime 19th-century house and garden is home to an eclectic eatery serving South East Asian fusion dishes, as well as more standard Romanian food. Great cocktails and a laid-back atmosphere make it ideal for serene summer evenings.

Nikos €€€ *Strada Nicolae Tonitza 6,* www.nikosgreektaverna.ro. This charming Greek restaurant leaves you feeling as if you've crossed into a parallel world – it wouldn't be out of place in Athens. Decorated to perfection, with old cans of olive oil hung from the ceiling an integral part of its charm, its seafood, lamb and fresh fish are a cut above the Bucharest average.

THE CIVIC CENTRE

Haute Pepper €€ *Bulevardul Unirii 2, tel: 072-628 4280,* www.hautepepper. ro. Located between the Palace of the Parliament and Piața Unirii, this is a modern, atmospheric space. They serve pretty much anything you could ask for, including seafood and a wide selection of pasta, alongside traditional and international dishes. The cocktails are great, too.

Stadio €€€ *Bulevardul Unirii 1, tel: 073-322 2220,* www.stadio.ro. Opposite Bucharest's parliament building, serving great food in a contemporary setting. Their grilled halloumi is a treat for vegetarians, and vegans will also be satisfied by the home-made hummus. Also simply a good spot for coffee on your way around.

CALEA VICTORIEI

Alt-Shift €€€ *Strada Constantin Mille 4, tel: 072-731 6245,* altshift.ro. Serving mainly Italian food as well as superior burgers and a cracking range of cocktails, this is a favourite for local hipsters. Reservations required.

Bistro Français €€€ *Strada Nicolae Golescu 18, tel: 074-208 0909,* www.bistro ateneu.ro. Contemporary takes on Romanian classics, such as nettle dumplings with crispy kale and zucchini, in Parisian-style surroundings; also offers an unparalleled selection of both old- and new-world wines.

Boutique du Pain €€ *Strada Academiei 28–30, tel: 072-844 3300,* https:// boutiquedupain.ro. Complete with tiled, checkerboard floor, this is a great café as well as a rather sophisticated bistro, where French food can be enjoyed in casual surroundings. The best onion soup in the city, and a mouthwatering assortment of home-made tartes.

Caju €€€ *Strada Nicolae Golescu 16, tel: 075-114 4545,* https://cajubyjoseph hadad.ro. A casual bistro on one of Bucharest's most Parisian-looking streets, Caju is picture-perfect and is where stylish locals come to feast on seafood and fine cuts of beef. There is plenty of North African influence too – not least the unsurpassable falafel and roasted eggplant with tahini – and a great wine list.

Camera din Față € *Strada D. I. Mendeleev 22,* www.cameradinfata.ro. Apothecary-like tearoom with a huge selection from around the globe – Darjeeling, Korea's Jeju Island, you name it. Also serves speciality coffee and a range of snacks.

Savart €€€ *Strada George Enescu nr. 2–4, tel: 074-357 5757,* www.savart.ro. This is one of Bucharest's most impressive restaurants, with dishes originating from all over the world; Moroccan salads, Indonesian soups, Basque burgers and Brazilian seafood stew, to name but a few, are delicious. Plenty of options for vegans, too.

The Artist €€€ *Calea Victoriei 147, tel: 072-831 8871,* www.theartist.ro. Romania's best fine-dining restaurant occupies an elegant villa, complete with an expansive garden in which they grow herbs. The Artist provides seasonal beauty on a plate, the tasting menus are great value and, for dessert, the signature cucumber sorbet is extraordinary.

AVIATORILOR AND HERĂSTRĂU PARK

18Lounge €€€ *City Gate (South Tower), Piața Presei Libere 3–5, tel: 073-350 1401,* www.18lounge.ro. This restaurant is on the 18th floor of an office building, so you can enjoy the food and drink with a sensational panoramic view. The tender, slow-roasted beef ribs served with pineapple and the crusted red tuna steak are top picks. Prices as high as the building, but worth the splurge.

Ancora €€€ *Șoseaua Nordului 7–9,* www.ancora-restaurant.ro. Quality seafood restaurant on the banks of Herăstrău Lake. Impressive in location and design, the menu features everything from sharing platters to stews and pasta dishes. All this does not come cheap, and it attracts a wealthy, local crowd.

Beans & Dots € *Bulevardul Primăverii 15,* www.beansanddots.ro. Attractive café on the ground level of the Museum of Recent Art; they also serve decent food.

Beraria H € *Șoseaua Pavel D. Kiseleff 32, tel: 072-534 5345,* www.berariah.ro. Claims to be the biggest beer hall in Europe, and it's difficult not to be convinced. Their simple yet tasty food includes a variety of tasty German sausages, huge pork knuckles; surprisingly, they've a pathetic range of draught beer. Live music most weekends, and it stays open late.

Ciorbarie € *Nicolae Titulescu 10,* www.ciorbarie.ro. The best of a handful of chains serving ciorba, the quintessential Romanian sour soup. There are always at least a dozen available, including vegan options, served with some of the best bread you will find in Bucharest. Other branches around the city.

Fior di Latte €€€ *Bulevardul Primăverii 19–21, tel: 078-442 0555,* www.fiordi latte.ro. Ideal if you are looking for high-end Italian food with an accent on seafood and fish, complemented by an amazing selection of Italian and French wines. The small raised terrace shows modern Bucharest at its best.

Kaiamo €€ *Strada Ermil Pangratti 30A, tel: 072-220 2204,* www.caiamo.com. Romanian food brought up to date by a highly-skilled, innovative young chef in a modern setting close to Herăstrău Park. If you ever wondered how pigs' trotters with caramelised cabbage or home-made ice cream with French fries might taste, this is the place to come.

Osho €€€ *Bulevardul Primăverii 19–21, tel: 021-568 3031,* www.osho-restaurant.ro. Fine cuts of beef and lamb from around the world, prepared in a variety of ways. Hugely popular with Bucharest's wealthy set, the restaurant offers a smart yet casual environment and an amazing burger.

COTROCENI AND CISMIGIU

Bocca Lupo €€ *Strada Doctor Joseph Lister 1, tel: 031-405 0050,* www.boccalupo.ro. Boasting a beautiful retro interior, this place serves supreme Italian food, with an array of imported hams, salamis and cheese. Favourites include the wood-fired pizza and fresh oysters, and the wine list is undeniably above the Bucharest average.

Jazz Book Bistro € *Strada Doctor Carol Davila 1, tel: 075-220 6746,* www.jazzbook.ro. Pizza, pasta, huge salads and lots of live jazz. It is exactly as aficionados like their jazz clubs: dark, a little seedy, but eclectic and lively, staffed and frequented by a great crowd of young locals looking for a different experience.

Kvala €€€ *Strada Doctor Louis Pasteur 63, tel: 072-673 1663,* www.kvala.ro. Greek restaurant and art gallery rolled into one – to put it in their own words, it's where 'fine taste meets fine taste.' The salads and seafood take top billing.

TRAVEL ESSENTIALS

PRACTICAL INFORMATION

A

ACCESSIBLE TRAVEL

Bucharest is improving access for travellers with disabilities but the city is still far from accessible for those with mobility difficulties. Even pushing a wheelchair on pavements is problematic, given the way that local drivers use them to park their cars. Buses and trams are ill-equipped, but almost all metro stations now have lifts. Some, but not all, museums are accessible and many larger hotels have some adapted rooms and wheelchair access.

ACCOMMODATION

Bucharest offers a wide range of accommodation for all budgets, from the very basic to luxury five-star hotels. There is also a good variety of private apartments available. Prices tend to be far lower than in most other European capitals at all levels. There is no real high or low season, although July and August tend to be quiet months as there are fewer business travellers in the city, and it's often very quiet early in the year. Weekends are invariably cheaper than weekdays.

I'd like a single/double room **Aş dori o cameră single/dublă**
with bath/shower **cu cadă/duş**
What's the rate per night? **Care este preţul pe noapte?**

AIRPORT

Bucharest's airport, **Henri Coanda International** (OTP; www.bucharest airports.ro), is north of the Romanian capital, 17km (11 miles) from the city centre. Most locals refer to it as Otopeni Airport. Bus #100 runs to the city centre (35min), and trains head to Gara de Nord (25min); both are 24 services, and from 2027 the metro's new Line 6 should also be an option. In theory, you can pay with contactless card, though this doesn't always work; paying by text message is an alternative. It is best to buy an Activ card, however (see page

119), which can then be used on public transport for the duration of your stay; 24hr and 72hr passes include all trains, buses, trams and metro services, and will suit most needs. Taxis can be ordered using the automatic machines in the arrivals hall; it takes 30–45 minutes to the city centre. The airport has been operating well over capacity for a number of years and can often be crowded, with long queues to pass through security and passport control – arrive well in advance of your flight.

Where can I get a taxi? **De unde pot lua un taxi?**
How much is it to downtown Bucharest? **Cât costă până în centrul Bucureștiului?**
Does this bus go to Bucharest? **Autobuzul acesta merge la București?**

C

CLIMATE

Bucharest is bitterly cold in winter, and swelters in July and August. The best weather is from April to May and September to October. June is the wettest month. Average daytime temperatures are as follows:

	Jan	Feb	Mar	Apr	May	June	July	Aug	Sep	Oct	Nov	Dec
°C	-2	2	7	11	17	20	22	21	18	12	5	1

CLOTHING

Romanians have few hang-ups about clothing, but you should note that many local women will cover their heads before entering churches; visitors are under no obligation to do the same, however. If invited into a Romanian home you should remove – or at least offer to remove – your footwear.

CRIME AND SAFETY

Bucharest is a pretty safe city. Violent crime is rare, and your most likely source of danger will be the pickpockets common on public transport, especially on routes to and from the airport and railway station. It's wise to make photocopies of travel documents and keep them in a separate place, such as a hotel safe. Theft should be reported in person to police; get a copy of your statement for your own insurance purposes. The emergency services phone number is 112.

E

ELECTRICITY

The current is 220 volts throughout Romania. You will need a two-pin adapter.

EMBASSIES AND CONSULATES

Australia: Strada Praga 3; tel: 037-406 0845; www.dfat.gov.au
Canada: Strada Tuberozelor 1–3; tel: 021-307 5000; www.international.gc.ca
Ireland: Strada Buzești 50–52; tel: 021-310 2131; www.ireland.ie/bucharest
South Africa: Strada Știrbei Vodă 26–28; tel: 021-313 3725; www.dirco.gov.za
UK: Strada Jules Michelet 24; tel: 021-201 7200; www.gov.uk
US: Bulevardul Dr. Liviu Librescu 4–6; tel: 021-200 3300; ro.usembassy.gov

EMERGENCIES

For all emergencies throughout Romania, call the general emergency number: 112.

G

GETTING THERE

Air travel. An increasingly large number of airlines fly from airports across the UK to Bucharest, including Wizz Air (www.wizzair.com), Ryanair (www.ryanair.com), British Airways (www.ba.com) and Tarom (www.tarom.ro). Fares can be very cheap. There are no direct flights to Bucharest from the US or Canada, but the city is well connected to Asia and Australia through Qatar Airways (www. qatarairways.com) and Turkish Airlines (www.turkishairlines.com).

Rail Travel. Bucharest can be reached by direct train from Vienna, Budapest, Sofia and Chişinău, and also Istanbul in summer only. There are no direct trains from the UK (the journey would include travelling via Paris and Vienna and then on to Bucharest, more than 48 hours); it's an expensive option suitable only for train buffs. InterRail (www.interrail.eu) and EurailPass (and its variants; www. eurail.com) are valid in Romania, though local fares are so cheap that you might as well not bother. All international trains arrive and depart from Gara de Nord.

By car/coach. Romania's lack of motorways means road trips through the country can be long and slow. If you plan to drive across the continent, the most direct route is via Ostend, Brussels, Cologne, Frankfurt, Vienna, Budapest and Oradea. Bucharest is 2,562km (1,592 miles) from London. Long distance buses are useful for trips to and from Sofia, as the journey time is shorter than the train. Flixbus (www.flixbus.com) operates buses to neighbouring countries, departing from Militari bus station (next to Pacii metro station).

GUIDES AND TOURS

There are numerous guided tours in Bucharest. Red Patrol (www.redpatrol. ro) offer communist-themed tours of the city in vintage Dacia cars, while Walkabout Free Tours (www.bucharest.walkaboutfreetours.com) runs a free, fun introduction to the city. Several agencies feature Bucharest on wider tours of Romania's Jewish heritage.

We'd like an English-speaking guide/an English interpreter **Am dori un ghid vorbitor de engleză/un traducător de engleză.**

H

HEALTH AND MEDICAL CARE

There are no specific health risks particular to Bucharest. Romanian doctors and healthcare professionals are highly skilled, and most speak English. The country's state-run hospitals in which they work are generally underfunded and run-down, however. The city's best, and most central, emergency hospital is Spitalul de Urgențe Floreasca (Calea Floreasca 8; tel: 021-599 2300), next to Stefan cel Mare metro station. All EU countries have reciprocal arrangements for healthcare. Emergency treatment is free for foreigners but you may be asked to pay for medicine; all other treatment has to be paid for when you receive the service. EU residents should obtain the European Health Insurance Card (EHIC), available from post offices or online (www.ehic.org.uk). This only covers medical care, not emergency repatriation costs or additional expenses. UK residents will need to check the latest regulations before travelling.

Tap water is not all that safe to drink, and the low cost of the bottled variety means that nobody actually does. Mosquitoes are a problem during the summer, and repellent is a must.

Pharmacies are ubiquitous (look for the sign *Farmacie*, usually written in green). Many stay open 24 hours.

> Where's the nearest (all night) pharmacy? **Unde este cea mai apropiată farmacie (cu program de noapte)?**
> I need a doctor/dentist **Am nevoie de un doctor/dentist**
> an ambulance **o ambulanță**
> hospital **spital**
> an upset stomach **durere de stomac**
> sunburn/a fever **insolație (arsură)/febră**

L

LANGUAGE

Romanian is a Latin language and is spoken by most of the population. Romanian's written form closely resembles French and Italian, and anyone with knowledge of those languages should get by. English is the foreign language of choice and most young people in Bucharest – and plenty of older ones – speak very good English.

There are some letters in the Romanian alphabet with no English equivalent:

Ă – pronounced as *er* in father

Â/Î – pronounced similarly to the *u* in lull

Ş – pronounced *sh* as in sheet

Ţ – pronounced *ts* as in tsar

LEFT LUGGAGE

There are left-luggage facilities (including self-service lockers) at Gara de Nord, but none at the airport.

LGBTQ TRAVELLERS

Bucharest's LGBTQ community is not yet wholly accepted by mainstream society. Bucharest Pride, which takes place in June, is an increasingly popular and well-attended event, however, and there is a lively gay club, **Q-Club**, (Bulevardul Carol I 61; www.theqclub.ro) open Thurs–Sat.

M

MEDIA

Magazines. The city guide *Bucharest In Your Pocket* (www.inyourpocket.com) has events listings information. Romania Insider (www.romania-insider.com) is a useful website which publishes news about Romania in English.

Television. TVR1 is the main state-run channel, with Pro TV the most popular private station. All Romanian TV stations include a lot of English-language programming, and as with films at the cinema, shows are usually subtitled, not dubbed.

MONEY

Romania's currency is the *leu*, plural *lei*. It is usually written in full (lei). Banknotes come in denominations of 500, 100, 50, 10, 5 and 1. One leu is subdivided into 100 bani, which comes in coins. Changing money is best done inside a bank, since exchange offices tend to charge exorbitant commissions and/or offer low rates of exchange. ATMs are everywhere, and credit and debit cards are accepted in almost all hotels, shops and restaurants. Holders of American Express and Diners Club cards may struggle.

Can I pay with this credit card? **Pot plăti cu cardul de credit?**
I want to change some pounds/dollars **Vreau să schimb niște lire sterline/dolari**
Where's the nearest bank/currency exchange office? **Unde e cea mai apropiată bancă/birou de schimb valutar?**
Is there an ATM near here? **Există un bancomat în apropiere?**
How much is that? **Cât costă?**

O

OPENING TIMES

Government offices, banks and other institutions tend to be open from 8.30am–4pm, Mon–Fri, usually without a pause for lunch. Museums have unpredictable opening hours, though tend to be variations on 10am–6pm. Most museums are closed Monday, some close Tuesday too.

Shops and supermarkets are open 9am–10pm. Almost all shops open on Sunday.

P

POLICE

If you need the police, call 112. Operators speak English, though the police force itself is notoriously mono-lingual. It also has a reputation for corruption, but you are only likely to encounter a policeman if driving, or if you seek one out for help. You should certainly not assume you can get out of trouble with a bribe, however, and take note that both drink driving and excessive speeding in theory both carry heavy prison sentences. As a rule you should carry some form of photo ID with you at all times, as this is law, but random checks are not common. A photocopy of your passport will suffice if you do not wish to carry the original around with you. The most central police station is at Strada Lascar Cartagiu 22, half way between Piaţa Romana and Piaţa Victoriei.

Where's the nearest police station? **Unde este cea mai apropiată staţie de poliţie?**
I've lost my... wallet/bag/passport **Mi-am pierdut... portofelul/ geanta/paşaportul**

POST OFFICES

Romanian post offices are slow, tortuous affairs where doing anything from buying a stamp to sending a parcel can take an age. Post boxes are usually only found directly outside post offices. For urgent letters and packets, DHL (www.logistics.dhl/ro-en) have offices across the city.

PUBLIC HOLIDAYS

Banks, post offices and any government office will be closed on public holidays. Orthodox Easter is the biggest celebration of the year, when much of the city will be closed, including large numbers of bars and restaurants.

1 January New Year's Day
24 January Principalities Day
April/May Orthodox Easter
1 May Labour Day
May/June Pentecost
1 June Children's Day
15 August Assumption of Mary
30 November St. Andrew
1 December National Day
25, 26 December Christmas

R

RELIGION

The vast majority of the Romanian population is Romanian Orthodox, similar in almost every way to the Orthodoxy practiced in Russia, Serbia, Bulgaria and Macedonia. Most churches hold services daily, with those on Sunday the best attended. Most worshippers stand (there are few seats in Romanian churches) and men and women stand separately: men on the right, women on the left. Women usually wear a headscarf.

T

TELEPHONES

Romania has four mobile networks: Vodafone (www.vodafone.ro), Orange (www.orange.ro), Digi Mobile (www.digiromania.ro) and T-Mobile (www.telekom.ro). All sell pre-pay cards, available from kiosks and most supermarkets, though for most roaming or an eSIM will suffice.

TIME ZONES

Romania is two hours ahead of Greenwich Mean Time (GMT+2). The chart below shows the times in Bucharest and other cities around the world:

New York	London	**Bucharest**	Sydney	Auckland
5am	10am	**12pm**	7pm	9pm

TIPPING

You are expected to tip waiters and waitresses in restaurants (though check your bill to ensure that service is not already included), where a 10 percent tip is seen as obligatory, regardless of whether you have been happy with the service. Unusually, taxi drivers in Bucharest do not expect to be tipped, and you should do so (2 or 3 lei) only if you have taken a taxi on a particularly short journey, in order to make the ride worth the driver's time and trouble.

TOILETS

There are very few public toilets in Bucharest. The most central are at Universitate metro station. There are portaloos in most of the city's parks, but these are best avoided. If you do get caught short, head for the nearest hotel or shopping centre.

Where are the toilets? **Unde este toaleta?**

TOURIST INFORMATION

Bucharest's official municipal tourist information centre is in the underpass at Universitate metro station (daily 10am–6pm; www.ampt.ro) and offers limited advice as well as maps and event information. Far better is the privately-run Bucharest Visitor Centre (Bulevardul Carol I 27, Mon–Fri 9am–5pm) which sells maps, city guides and organises tours of the city as well as excursions around the country.

TRANSPORT

Bucharest has an extensive public transport system comprising of metro lines, trams, buses and trolley-buses. The system serves every part of the city, but few of its outskirts. Current fares and route information can be found at www.stbsa.ro (for trams, buses and trolley-buses) and www.metrorex.ro (for the metro).

Most public transport runs from 5am to 11.30pm, although some lines stop running a little earlier. There is a good range of night buses, all of which depart from Piața Unirii.

Tickets. There are a bewildering number of tickets and passes available for Bucharest's various forms of public transport. You can choose to pay per journey – tickets can be bought at kiosks next to most bus and tram stops, as well as at the entrance to the metro, and contactless payment is also possible (though there have been teething problems on the buses). Many travellers will be better off buying a 24hr or 72hr Activ card, valid on all services; cards including transport from the airport are more expensive. There are also day passes for both buses and the metro system. Ticket inspectors, wearing blue vests marked *control*, hand out on-the-spot fines to fare dodgers.

Taxis. Bucharest's official taxis have a poor reputation, and are best avoided: while fares are nominally cheap, drivers often refuse to use the meter and instead insist on a flat fare often many times higher. **Uber** (www.uber.com) and **Bolt** (www.bolt.eu) are better choices for those with smartphones, or ask your hotel or restaurant to call a taxi from a reputable company.

Scooters. Electric scooters belonging to **Lime** (www.li.me) and **Bolt** (www. bolt.eu) can be found scattered all over the city centre and make a good alternative to other forms of transport for short distances; the former can be booked using the Uber app.

Where can I get a taxi? **De unde pot lua un taxi?**
What's the fare to ... ? **Cât costă biletul până la ...?**
Where is the nearest bus stop? **Unde e cea mai apropiată stație de autobuz?**
When's the next bus to ...? **Când este următorul autobuz pentru ...?**
I want a ticket to ... **Vreau un bilet la ...**
single/return **dus/dus și întors**
Will you tell me when to get off? **Puteți să-mi spuneți când să cobor?**

V

VISAS AND ENTRY REQUIREMENTS

Romania is not yet part of the Schengen area, but follows its rules. EU and EEA passport holders can enter without a visa, and stay as long as they please. Citizens of the US, Canada, Australia and New Zealand (and, in fact, most American or Oceanian nations) can enter the country visa-free and stay for up to 90 days. South Africans, and citizens of most other countries, need to procure a visa from a Romanian consulate abroad before travelling.

If exporting antiques, you should check with the shop you are purchasing from to find out if the object is deemed part of the country's national heritage. If so, you will need a special permit to take it out of the country. All good antique dealers can arrange the paperwork.

W

WEBSITES

The following websites may be useful:

www.cfrcalatori.ro/en The official site of Romanian Railways (CFR), including online ticket purchase.

www.inyourpocket.com A thorough guide to Bucharest (and many other Romanian cities), including up-to-date event information.

www.mae.ro/en The foreign ministry's official website, which includes up-to-date visa and travel information.

www.romania-insider.com News about Bucharest and Romania in English.

www.romania.travel The official website of the Romanian tourist office includes a good section dedicated to Bucharest.

www.stbsa.ro Bucharest's public transport operator, including timetables.

Y

YOUTH HOSTELS

Bucharest has a wide range of private youth hostels, though no national hostelling association exists. Despite a young crowd, most hostels operate a 16s-and-over policy. Below are two popular options:

First Hostel (Bulevardul Mărăşeşti 86; www.firsthostel.ro) is just south of Piaţa Unirii and while not inviting from the outside, has some comfortable and colourful dorms and private rooms.

Popcorn Hostel (Strada Pisoni 26; www.popcornhostel.ro) has good dorms as well as private rooms; it's right next to Gara de Nord, making it perfect for early or late trains. Unlimited free popcorn.

WHERE TO STAY

Hotels in Romania are graded from one to five stars. The choice of visitor accommodation in Bucharest has always been excellent; competition, as well as relatively low local wages, keeps prices down, and while accommodation is likely to be your biggest expense in the city, the cost is generally cheaper than most European capitals.

There is no real high season in Bucharest, and there is usually a variety of rooms available, even at the last minute. However, some of the most popular hotels in the city are small, quirky affairs which are sold out months in advance: those places are noted in the listings as needing to be booked well ahead of time.

The following guide denotes the rack rate price of a double room during the week, including breakfast and tax. Hotel room rates in Romania, especially at the upper end, are almost always quoted in euros.

€€€	**Over 150 euros**
€€	**75–150 euros**
€	**Under 75 euros**

PIAȚA UNIVERSITĂȚII AND THE OLD TOWN

Europa Royale €€ *Strada Franceză 60, tel: 021-319 1798,* www.europaroyale bucharest.com. Located opposite the Old Court Church, where Bucharest was founded, this is a beautifully renovated,19th-century building, serving as a comfortable and well-priced hotel. Bags of character, and views over Piața Unirii from some of the rooms, most of which are enormous.

Grand €€€ *Bulevardul Nicolae Bălcescu 4, tel: 021-310 2020,* www.grandhotel bucahrest.ro. Bucharest's first five star hotel, this Modernist high-rise has had a front row seat for all of the prominent events in the city over the past 40 years. Boasts a swimming pool and sun terrace on the top floor.

Hemingway Residence €€ *Strada Mantuleasa 31, tel: 021-312 1092,* www. hemingwayresidence.ro. These luxury apartments are located close to Piața

Universității, at prices far lower than most luxury hotels. The larger apartments are ideal for families, with separate bedrooms and fully equipped kitchens. Unlike many short-term apartment lets, staff are on-site 24 hours a day.

PeakTure €€ *Strada Slănic 26, tel: 021-302 9280,* www.peakture.ro. Found on a secluded side street, although just a few steps from the bustling Piața Universității, is this small yet elegant hotel; it offers luxurious accommodation at an affordable price, with contemporary interior flourishes that complement the traditional exterior.

Rembrandt €€ *Strada Smârdan 11, tel: 072-735 3393,* www.rembrandt.ro. Arguably the most sought-after hotel in the Old Town of Bucharest, originally a merchant townhouse, now beautifully restored. The few rooms are all fabulously designed, complete with gorgeous, original wooden flooring from the 19th century. Reserve well in advance.

THE CIVIC CENTRE

CH €€ *Bulevardul Mircea Vodă 21, tel: 021-300 0545,* www.hotelchbucharest.com. Perfect for visitors looking to explore the nearby old Jewish district, this is a large, modern hotel, characterised by glass, steel and sharp lines. The first-class staff make it a home from home for guests.

Grand Pier Boutique Villa €€ *Calea Șerban Vodă 22–24, tel: 074-217 0764,* https://grandpierboutique.ro. Just behind Piața Unirii, offering lavishly decorated rooms, all individually designed with plenty of flair and featuring traditional furniture, plush carpets and contemporary touches. Some rooms are quite small, but they're priced accordingly.

JW Marriott €€€ *Calea 13 Septembrie 90, tel: 021-403 0000,* www.marriott.com/hotels/travel/buhro-jw-marriott-bucharest-grand-hotel. This enormous hotel was built at the same time as the Parliament, part of the Civic Centre. Architecturally outstanding, its interiors feature marble at every turn, huge rooms, fabulous onsite dining and shopping, and an indoor swimming pool.

Parliament € *Strada Izvor 106, tel: 021-411 9990,* http://parliament-hotel.ro. While the Parliament building is visible from most parts of the city, from this hotel the view is incomparable. Although not immediately attractive from the outside, its agreeable interior offers rooms which are all spacious and bright, decorated in soothing, pastel shades, and have large windows to admire one of the best views in Bucharest.

Suter Palace €€€ *Aleea Suter 23–25, tel: 031-710 1113,* www.suterpalace. com. Secluded luxury in a private setting that is as close to get-away-from-it-all as you will find in Bucharest. There are just 17 rooms and suites; all are exquisitely decorated with fine furniture and fittings that incorporate many original elements of the palace, notably the fireplaces. The private garden and terrace are also wonderful.

CALEA VICTORIEI

Barrio € *Strada Biserica Amzei 3, tel: 073-433 3020,* www.barrio.ro. This elegant Art Nouveau house was once the home of a well-known Romanian literary family, and has been converted into a decently priced hotel. It offers just eight rooms, a couple of which are set over two levels and are rather special. The location is next to one of the busiest markets in the city and close to plenty of bars and restaurants.

Casa Capsa €€ *Calea Victoriei 36, tel: 021-313 4038,* www.capsa.ro. Historic hotel, dating back to the 1860s, with a coffee house that was for decades a popular literary hub. Casa Capsa has been renovated to the highest standards but still retains its original charm, from the wrought iron lamps at the entrance to the wonderful interior courtyard.

Grand Hotel Continental €€€ *Calea Victoriei 56, tel: 037-201 0300,* https:// grand-hotel-continental-bucuresti.continentalhotels.ro. More than two centuries of history are packed into this hotel, which in 1995 hosted the former king of Romania, Mihai, who addressed a crowd of almost a million people from its balcony. Classy rooms and suites, fine dining and great service make it more comfortable and homely than its grand size would suggest.

Hello € *Calea Griviței 143, tel: 037-212 1800,* www.hellohotels.ro. Hello is just about the cheapest non-hostel sleep in the city, and is located opposite Bucharest's main railway station, Gara de Nord. Rooms and bathrooms are tiny but modern, well-equipped and impeccably clean. For a short stay they are perfect for anyone on a budget. Breakfast not included.

InterContinental Athénée Palace €€€ *Strada Episcopiei 1–3, tel: 021-303 3777,* www.atheneepalace-hotel.ro. From the marble colonnade that greets you on entry to the sumptuous rooms, many of which have magnificent views over Piața Revoluției towards the former Royal Palace, this property oozes luxury and history and is not without its intrigue. Its English Bar – which has a starring role in Olivia Manning's Balkan Trilogy – is a Bucharest legend, little changed in a century.

Moxa € *Strada Mihail Moxa nr 2–4, tel: 021-650 5555,* https://hotelmoxa.com. In a prime location on the northern, residential end of Calea Victoriei, this hotel is a beautifully restored mansion house. Moxa offers spacious, high-ceilinged rooms with views of the lively street below. The bathrooms are particularly stylish, and the buffet breakfast is one of the finest in the city.

Radisson Blu €€€ *Calea Victoriei 63–81, 021-311 9000,* www.radissonhotels.com/en-us/hotels/radisson-blu-bucharest. While not packing the historical punch of the more famous Athénée Palace opposite, this luxury hotel offers both indoor and outdoor pools, and can boast one of the most jaw-dropping lobbies in Bucharest – a gem of contemporary design.

AVIATORILOR AND HERĂSTRĂU PARK

Arc de Triomphe €€ *Strada Clucerului 19, tel: 021-223 1978,* https://hotelarcdetriomphe.ro. Situated in one of the leafiest areas of the city, an elegant villa offering large rooms of excellent value and tremendous customer service. You can relax in the spa, complete with plunge pool, sauna and jacuzzi, and dine with wonderful views at the rooftop restaurant.

M-Point Motel € *Strada Clucerului 21, tel: 073-226 1941,* https://m-point-motel.business.site. Simple yet charming and quirky rooms, with beamed ceilings and inventive use of space. Some rooms are on the small side and there is little in the way of extras, but located in an upmarket residential area, and great value for money.

Pensiunea Helvetia € *Strada Popa Savu 75, tel: 021-223 0566*. This little place has been offering good accommodation at little expense since the 1990s. Although located opposite the main entrance to Herăstrău Park, its rooms nevertheless provide one of the most peaceful sleeps in the city. The breakfast is amazing, and the staff – many who have worked here for years – are tremendously helpful.

Pullman €€€ *Piața Montreal 10, tel: 021-318 3000,* all.accor.com. Upmarket hotel towering over Piața Presei Libere, and offering big rooms with wonderful views of Herăstrău Park from the upper floors. Part of the Bucharest World Trade Center, and enormously popular with business travellers. The bus to and from the airport stops right outside.

Triumf € *Strada Șoseaua Pavel D. Kiseleff 12,* www.hoteltriumf.ro. Basically the Grand Bucharest Hotel – Wes Anderson would love this large 1930s pile, which though creaking at the seams exudes a singular kind of charm (check out the chandeliers in the always-empty restaurant). Rates are often an absolute steal.

Vila Paris €€ *Strada Paris 58, tel: 021-231 3151,* www.vilaparis.ro. With traditional decor, reproduction period furniture and huge windows providing ample light, this place is a prime choice in Bucharest. The location is great, close to a number of lovely restaurants and a short walk from the metro. There are just nine rooms and the hotel can often be full, so it is recommended to reserve well in advance.

COTROCENI AND CISMIGIU

Cismigiu €€ *Bulevardul Regina Elisabeta 38, tel: 031-403 0500,* www.hotel cismigiu.ro. An impressive Art-Nouveau building dating from 1912, exemplifying how history and contemporary design can be fused to breathe life into a city landmark. The beer hall on the ground floor is as long-standing and famous as the hotel, which became the subject of a song by local band, Vama.

Epoque €€ *Intrarea Aurora 17C, tel: 021-312 3232,* www.hotelepoque.ro. A stunning, imposing – yet refined – neo-Romanian exterior prefaces the interior of this hotel, which has abundant stylish features. Located close to the city centre and the glorious Cismigiu Park, its setting in a cul-de-sac offers a quiet retreat from the busy heart of the city. One of the few city centre hotels to offer a swimming pool.

Siqua €€ *Calea Plevnei 59A, tel: 021-319 5160*. Set behind the Bucharest National Opera House, and a great option for those looking for a relatively upmarket stay at an affordable price. The rooms are large and elegantly decorated with colourful murals, and the small garden terrace is a wonderful place to eat breakfast.

Trianon € *Strada Grigore Cobălcescu 9, 021-311 4927,* www.hoteltrianon.ro. Just a few steps from Cismigiu Park, in one of the few Secession-style buildings in Bucharest, built at the beginning of the 20th century. There are 42 vibrantly decorated yet tasteful rooms and, given the brilliant location, the prices are an absolute steal.

Venezia € *Strada Pompiliu Eliade 2, tel: 021-310 6872,* www.hotelvenezia.ro. On a very busy square halfway between Cismigiu Park and the Opera House, a unique, curved shape creates quirky spaces and ensures that each room is both unique and charming. This hotel is a perfect choice if you want direct access to a variety of shops, bars, restaurants and clubs.

INDEX

THE **MINI** ROUGH GUIDE TO
BUCHAREST

Second edition 2024

Editor: Siobhan Warwicker
Author: Sophie Radford
Updater: Martin Zatko
Picture Editor: Tom Smyth
Cartography Update: Carte
Layout: Grzegorz Madejak
Head of DTP and Pre-Press: Rebeka Davies
Head of Publishing: Sarah Clark
Photography Credits: iStock 4TL, 5T, 5T, 6B, 11, 13, 14, 17, 19, 32, 33, 35, 37, 38, 42, 44, 47, 51, 52, 56, 57, 58, 61, 63, 66, 68, 69, 70, 73, 76, 79, 80, 82, 88, 89, 92, 93, 96, 100; Library of Congress 22; Shutterstock 1, 4ML, 5M, 5T, 6T, 7B, 7T, 21, 25, 27, 28, 30, 40, 41, 43, 48, 54, 59, 64, 74, 84, 86, 95, 99
Cover Credits: The National Library Shutterstock

Distribution

UK, Ireland and Europe: Apa Publications (UK) Ltd; sales@roughguides.com
United States and Canada: Ingram Publisher Services; ips@ingramcontent.com
Australia and New Zealand: Booktopia; retailer@booktopia.com.au
Worldwide: Apa Publications (UK) Ltd; sales@roughguides.com

Special Sales, Content Licensing and CoPublishing
Rough Guides can be purchased in bulk quantities at discounted prices. We can create special editions, personalised jackets and corporate imprints tailored to your needs. sales@roughguides.com; http://roughguides.com
All Rights Reserved
© 2024 Apa Digital AG
License edition © Apa Publications Ltd UK
Printed in Czech Republic
This book was produced using **Typefi** automated publishing software.

Contact us
Every effort has been made to provide accurate information in this publication, but changes are inevitable. The publisher cannot be held responsible for any resulting loss, inconvenience or injury sustained by any traveller as a result of information or advice contained in the guide. We would appreciate it if readers would call our attention to any errors or outdated information, or if you feel we've left something out. Please send your comments with the subject line "Rough Guide Mini Bucharest Update" to mail@uk.roughguides.com.